Accidental Sisters

The Story of My 52 Year Wait to Meet My Biological Sibling

Katherine Linn Caire

ISBN: 978-1-95386557-1 (Paperback)
ISBN: 978-1-95386558-8 (eBook)

Library of Congress Control Number: 00000000000

Books Fluent
3014 Dauphine Street
New Orleans, LA
70117

To my husband, Don; daughters Lauren, Carolyn, and Kat; my brand-spanking-new son-in-law, Doug; and of *course*, my sister Marcia.

Also:

To the little girl out there—soon to be born but not just yet—who will not comprehend the tenuous situation that she is in on the day that she enters this earthly world. Be comforted in knowing that although the time will not be right for your birth mother to raise you, your mother, who is not biologically linked to you, will come along at the perfect moment and will become your bridge, your launching pad. Be assured that all is divinely orchestrated.

Contents

Author's Note / 7

Prologue / 9

CHAPTER 1   Prayers Answered / 13

CHAPTER 2   A Fateful Search / 27

CHAPTER 3   A Series of Fortunate Events / 63

CHAPTER 4   Getting Acquainted / 81

CHAPTER 5   Meet You at the Baggage Claim / 91

CHAPTER 6   "New" Sisters / 97

CHAPTER 7   Meeting Margaret Maurer / 109

CHAPTER 8   Questions Unanswered / 119

CHAPTER 9   Loss and Revelation / 135

CHAPTER 10   Arizona Bound / 149

CHAPTER 11   Maurer Territory / 161

CHAPTER 12   Synchropregnicity / 169

CHAPTER 13   Facing the Unknown / 177

CHAPTER 14   Moving On / 201

Acknowledgments / 213

Author's Note

This book is a true story based on knowledge provided by a number of sources, not just my sister and me. I was extremely fortunate to be given copies of my birth mother's journals, which filled in several previous gaps. I conducted interviews whenever I had the luck to be able to speak to someone still living who was directly involved in the story. In many instances, I conducted research in order to put pieces of the puzzle together. The story of my adoption was well known in our family, as the circumstances, being unusual, caused people to ask my parents about it dozens of times over the years, multiple times in my presence.

Actual names have been used, with the exception of a few individuals who I was not able to make contact with to ask for their permission to be included. It was also necessary to plug in pseudonyms of people who were part of this story, whose actual names remain unknown. One name was changed just because it was the right thing to do.

It took time and patience to put it all together, but I loved the whole process. Adoption is a beautiful thing for many reasons, but I hope that you will agree even more so after reading our story. I am thrilled that you are here, on this page, about to embark on my journey with me!

Prologue

I did not know that I'd actually been waiting for fifty-two years. My parents had adopted me at birth, my brother Jamie almost four years later. I'd known that we were adopted; Mom and Dad explained it to me even when I was probably too young to understand. Once Jamie was old enough, they did the same for him. Thus, from toddler years until the days that I unbearably lost both of my adoptive parents a little over three years apart, in my mind they were my God-given parents and my brother was meant to be my only sibling.

I knew from a fairly young age that I was very fortunate to have such loving parents and grandparents and that my situation could have been very different from what it was. Mom and Dad's tight, decades-long friendship with three other couples in Des Moines created an extended family, adding what amounted to three additional pairs of aunts and uncles and ten extended siblings. In my mind, my family wasn't just the four of us Linns. The brood extended to and included the Adrianses, the Hempelmans, and the Longeneckers. We spent all our years growing up celebrating holidays together, going on summer and fall day-long picnics with all four families, taking hundreds of swimming lessons from the Hempelman children, learning all sorts of tricks on the trampoline from the Longenecker children, and playing endless hours of hide-and-seek in the Adrianse house, which had the *best* nooks and crannies for hiding of any house I'd ever been in. My brother Jamie and I were two of the three youngest in this mélange of twelve children, so all these activities were even more exciting for us. I won the adoption lottery, and I knew it.

For over five decades, I never felt like anyone was missing. Of course, I knew that I had birth parents out there somewhere, but I didn't think much about them because my adoptive parents, Ruth and Chuck Linn, were the guardians of my soul, protectors of my being. But as I have learned, sometimes there is a shift—when it's happening you may not know why, but it is critical to pay attention. It can come out of nowhere and hit you over the head like a ton of bricks.

Someone encouraged me that night, late at night during the spring of 2012, to contact Catholic Charities in Des Moines where I was adopted shortly after birth. The odd thing is that finding out *any* information about my birth parents had never even been on my radar or of any interest to me—until that night. Then suddenly, while thinking about something completely unrelated, a new thought floated into my head, urging me to ask for a social/medical search with my birth records so that my three daughters would have more than just 50 percent of their medical histories. It seemingly came out of nowhere, but I knew better than to ignore it. I needed to pay attention, and find out where this was leading me. By this time in my life, I knew how to discern the difference between my own ponderings versus messages that came to me from outside my brain.

The information contained in the social/medical search was and is very important, but it wasn't until months later that I found out that that first message was just the catalyst to get me going in the right direction. Someone on the other side, possibly my birth mother, perhaps my guides, knew it was time to get me rolling before it was too late. Unbeknownst to me, I had a sister to find.

At the end of this book, I've included my birth mother's perspective regarding the events that surround her pregnancy with me and my birth. While informed by history, this part of her story is predominantly conjured from my own imagination. When I was in the midst of writing other chapters, my oldest daughter Lauren and I took a walk. She suggested that I not only write about this narrative from my family's perspective but also from my birth mother's. This caused me to spend a good deal of time in deep thought about what my birth mother went through during that period, and more importantly, how she felt. I believe that *that* was the first time I truly attempted to analyze all that it took for her to get through her pregnancy with me, to give birth to me, and to move on. In the past, I'd wondered what exactly transpired in the months leading up to my birth and adoption, although I never thought it out in great detail. Now I was contemplating what it must have been like for her, what she felt, how she handled it and, ultimately, what she regretted.

Due to the lucky fortune of meeting immediate biological family members who could fill in the details, combined with actual written information from my birth mother, both in saved memorabilia and journals, I was able to fill in a lot of blanks. The rest of her chapter is filled with my wonderings and imagination.

CHAPTER 1

Prayers
Answered

T he story of my adoption was something that I heard many times over the course of my childhood and even into early adulthood. It was retold again and again by my dad whenever someone asked, with my mom chiming in here and there for good measure. I wish that I could hear the story again in Dad's voice, just one more time. As that isn't possible, I will tell you about this most significant day in my life as best as I know how to, in his style, in his way. I want you to have the opportunity to know about these loving people who became my parents on that very special day.

As described by my dad, Charles Gilcrest Linn, the waits in between sightings felt painful and endless. This was the first trip of this nature for him. It was October 1959, and he was experiencing it with three of his best friends from Des Moines. He and my mom had moved to the capital city of Iowa when he became employed by the family lumber business six years before. The two of them had traveled a bit during their first half-dozen years of marriage, but to date, neither of them had been to Canada. The Canadian wilderness had my father awestruck by its beauty and boundlessness.

Dad recalled that moose hunting was the furthest thing from his mind when his good friend Ben asked him to join the group for this adventure. He was not a hunter in the classic sense; he had never gone out to hunt any animal. However, this was a group of his inner circle—some of his very best friends on this planet. He sensed that the trip was a lot more about male bonding than it was about doing anything other than enjoying the exquisite majesty of a moose.

The weather that day was quite typical of autumn there; it was cool and crisp, comfortable in the sun and chilly in the woods. They moved through the forest after having no success at sightings for hours. Their guide found a new area where they were well concealed and they proceeded to plant themselves, ready for the next survey. They were sitting quietly on the wait when they heard the oncoming sound of hooves traversing through the woods. My dad knew that the hooves they heard crushing down upon the fallen leaves and the dry, compacted soil did not sound like those of a moose. Much lighter, defter. Too swift and nimble to be an animal of that size.

Dad looked over his shoulder and was surprised to see the well-known majestic red jackets in the distance, bobbing up and down on the backs of two equine escorts. The Royal Canadian Mounted Police (RCMP), known as the "Mounties," were and still are the federal and national police force of Canada. Its jurisdiction over federal law enforcement in Canada during the late 1950s was vast and included all provinces in Canada except for Ontario and Quebec.

As Dad recalled, he nudged his buddy Mark to point out the approaching horsemen, his mind frantically wandering, trying to figure out why the Mounties were heading toward their group. As he said, they were just four guys from Des Moines, Iowa, on a men's sightseeing trip, trying to get away and relax for a while. Considering the breadth of the RMCP's responsibilities, Dad found his heart rate picking up considerably, wondering if they were about to be mistakenly accused of drug trafficking, illegal entry, counterfeiting, or some other weighty organized crime.

He found it odd that their guide seemed not the least bit concerned, as if the Mounties showing up were as common as the sun appearing in the sky each day. The four Americans were frozen, most likely with all their mouths hanging open, transfixed by the two Mounties as they finally approached the group.

The Mountie closest to them, now just a dozen feet away, addressed the group. "Which of you gentlemen is Charles Gilcrest Linn from Des Moines, Iowa?"

That would be my dad.

He wanted to respond but wasn't able to immediately. As the Mounties slowed down and rode up to the group, my poor father had dozens of conflicting thoughts rushing through his head as to what he might have possibly done wrong to invite the presence of these authorities. He said that amongst these racing thoughts was a panicked checklist of all the things he had done in his life that might be considered ill-conceived at best. He honestly felt like he'd lived a clean life and that the list that he was trying to conjure up was none too exciting. As the mangled panic of thoughts sloshed around in his head, he finally forced a response out of his parched throat.

"I am Charles Linn."

"Okay, Mr. Linn. We will need for you to come back to our headquarters for a very important phone call."

Six Hours Earlier

My mom, Ruth Ann Linn, loved the time of the year in Des Moines when fall finally decided to make its appearance. Most people had had enough of the heat and humidity of August when an occasional cool, crisp day would begin to tease Iowans in September. Once October arrived, it was truly fall, with stunning changes in the leaves' colors and frosts greeting all upon awakening. Mom always took this change in weather as an invitation to spend even more time in her beloved gardens.

Mom had been home alone for almost a week, because my crazy dad had agreed to go on a moose expedition in Canada with three of his dearest, most profligate friends. Mom and Dad had been married just over six years and Mom had worked as a secretary at a car dealership in Des Moines until 1956. After they had saved up enough to start building their little house on Gilmore Avenue, they made the decision that Mom would stay home and they would try to start a family. They had already been trying to have a baby for years before the move, but had experienced no luck.

Mom had expressed her concerns to her gynecologist, Dr. Moore, and he had gently explained that this could well have something to do with the poison that had spread rampantly through her body back when she was twenty years old. She was one of those rare patients whose appendix ruptured with no associated pain. She had walked around for what doctors later estimated was over a day, unaware of the danger lurking inside of her body, when she suddenly collapsed in the street. She was rushed to the hospital, so gravely ill that the doctors were sure that she wouldn't survive. Mom recalled many times how Dad sat by her bedside religiously, willing her to choose life. That was when Dad told her that he wanted to marry her. That brush with death made her realize the importance of the resolve to live and what an impact those who love you can have on your decision to fight.

So, there my mother was, years into trying to have a baby and attempting to stay positive about the whole process, but, in her mind, every month that went by with no pregnancy meant that having a baby was all the more unlikely. Her heartache as she watched her closest friends and relatives have one baby after another must have been a despair that I will never fully comprehend. One time when I was younger and my mom talked about it, she used the term *barren* to describe her lack of ability to conceive. I had to leave the room and go to my bedroom to cry my eyes out for her; it was one of the saddest terms that I'd ever heard. Dad stayed very optimistic—or, at least, that was the show that he put on to protect Mom. He was definitely her tower of strength through the rollercoaster of emotions that plagued her during those years.

They knew that they wanted children no matter what, so they'd made the decision years ago to apply to adopt a baby through Catholic Charities in Des Moines. They decided that if they became pregnant sometime after the application, that was fine too . . . they just wanted to make sure that all options for welcoming a child into their home were open. The adoption journey was uncharted territory for my parents; none of their relatives or closest friends up to that point in their lives had gone through the process. I think that Mom and Dad were both hoping and praying that those changes—a move to their first family house and Mom's staying home and focusing on more domestic issues—would create a healthier mindset for the start of their eventual family. Whether that involved them having biological children or adopting them, Mom and Dad were determined to make it work out.

It was the morning of October 16, 1959. Mom was engaged in her usual morning chores at home and had just come inside from watering their front and back gardens. Georgie, our beloved dachshund, always followed her around as she spent time in her gardens. This morning was no different, as Georgie came waddling in behind her, slightly damp from imposing herself between the hose and the plants. It was a habit that caused Mom to always have an old, worn out "dog towel" on the dryer in the laundry room, knowing that the wet, bristling black hair was most likely to occur after a morning trip around the house. As she grabbed the ratty white towel, she turned to see Ditto, our silver tabby, sitting in the middle of the kitchen floor staring at her. Ditto was aptly named because when Mom and Dad adopted her, she had been having one litter of kittens after another, so the previous owner decided that name fit her much better than her original, predictable moniker: Kitty. Her glare when breakfast was even a moment late on any given morning was one of her trademarks.

Mom wiped down Georgie's gleaming coat of ink-black hair, then went to the fridge and pulled out both Georgie's and Ditto's food. As was always the case, both animals inhaled their bowls of food as soon as they hit the floor. Neither one of them ever missed a meal, and the food was usually devoured in less than a few minutes.

She opened the dishwasher to pull out a clean bowl and glass for her own breakfast. It had been quiet the last few mornings without Dad around, scrambling through their usual morning routines before he left for the lumber company. Vacation time for Dad without Mom along was a very rare occurrence, but Mom knew he needed it. He had always given his all at Gilcrest Lumber, since he first began working there. It was a small business that had been in the family since 1856. Dad felt an immense pride in being a part of it and its continuity. I think that it had a lot to do with him wanting the company to continue to remain successful and grow; there is a sense of ownership that may be a bit stronger when someone is involved in a family commodity business. Gilcrest had already stood the test of time with its forefathers generations ahead of Dad. He experienced a rather unique pressure, self-imposed, in knowing that the company had been in business for over one hundred years.

Just as Mom was about to eat her breakfast, the phone rang. Of course, in 1959, there were only landlines. No cell phones, no caller ID, just a simple black phone hanging on the kitchen wall.

Mom answered and the voice on the other end was one she had not heard for quite some time. Each and every time that she had spoken with this kind lady before, Mom ran through the full gamut of emotions, from the utmost hopeful anticipation to the depths of despair.

"Mrs. Linn, it is so good to talk to you again. This is Erica at Catholic Charities. I know it's been a while since we talked. I have some really wonderful news for you . . . do you have time to talk?

"Yes, of course!" Mom responded. As my mother told me, no matter how long it had been since she heard from Erica, her heart always skipped a beat when she called again.

Erica wasted no time. "Your day has finally arrived. You and Mr. Linn have a baby daughter!"

Mom had guessed this was just another 'update' call. Her knees quivered and her mouth was parched—but in all the best ways possible. She and Dad had waited for this moment for just over four years, ever since they had first decided to adopt a child. Her mind's eye suddenly flashed to the small bedroom in their house that had been set up long ago as a nursery—a beautiful family crib with its tender bedding, matching curtains framing the one window in that room, gentle light spilling onto the furniture, waiting to caress their newborn. All of these facets of one room, sitting so lonely for so long, pensive and waiting . . . until now!

"I know that you've been hanging in there for a long time, but you still must be quite shocked by this sudden news. Mrs. Linn, that is completely normal. Please call Mr. Linn, take your time, and then let me know what time you two would like to come over to Christ

Child Home to see her. Your daughter is a healthy little girl, born here in Des Moines in September. She is very much looking forward to meeting her parents!"

"Erica, I'm afraid I can't call my husband right now," Mom explained. "He is in the middle of the Canadian wilderness on a sightseeing trip, but will be home in two days. May I come and meet our baby this afternoon by myself?"

This is where things got weird.

"Mrs. Linn . . . are you and Mr. Linn still married?"

Although Mom found it difficult to utter anything, she managed, "Of course we are! Why would you ask that?"

"Mrs. Linn, we will need both parents to be present for the adoption and official delivery. We do not allow adoptions with single mothers, nor do we allow exchanges with just the mother."

Erica's abrupt turn in demeanor completely threw my mother off and threw me for a loop the first time Mom told me about the conversation. Then I remembered all the reading I had been doing about adoption in America and why many agencies had decided to follow very strict guidelines to avoid (what they considered to be) potentially dangerous situations for the babies or children. As backward as that seems today, that's just how it was back in 1959.

That moment was when my mom knew she needed to get in touch with my dad as soon as possible.

❀ ❀ ❀

On the relatively brief trip back to their headquarters, Dad found it peculiar that these two Mounties were so lighthearted—joking with each other and laughing it up, but not talking to Dad at all. He wondered . . . was this their sick way of scaring him even more? Arresting him for something he didn't do, or even more convoluted, maybe he was breaking a law in Canada that he had no idea was actually a law. The other concern that plagued him was, why a phone call? Dad wished he knew. His mind was racing all over the place, his imagination on steroids. His nervous, flawed reasoning kept conjuring up images of being in jail in a foreign country, and worse. He needed to find a way to stop and breathe.

Once they arrived at the base, Dad was so exhausted from his mind continually racing that he just wanted to get it over with, whatever that meant. He was alone with these strangers and his three buddies were presumably still back in the woods. Within a matter of minutes, the Mounties had him sitting behind an ordinary, unadorned wooden desk with yet another man that he didn't know staring back at Dad, holding the receiver of an old black phone out toward my father.

"Mr. Linn, good afternoon. Glad you could make it in because it is a *very* good day for you! Someone on the other end is especially eager to speak with you!"

As soon as he put the receiver to his ear, Dad could hear the familiar static of a long-distance phone call. After he said hello, he took in the sound of someone in the midst of a muffled, delicate cry on the other end of the line . . . which quickly turned into an all-out sob. Dad, of course, knew exactly who it was. It was his dear wife, my precious soon-to-be mother, and something was terribly wrong.

There was a brief, faint, "Chuck—" that Mom muttered on the other end. Then more sobs followed. Dad's heart began to race again, feeling sure that she was calling to tell him that someone they dearly loved had perished. He felt utterly helpless being so far away from her.

"Oh my gosh, dear . . . what is wrong?"

"Nothing is wrong, Chuck. This is an incredible, miraculous day. Sorry to shorten your trip, but please get home as soon as possible. We have a new baby daughter to pick up!"

CHAPTER 2

A Fateful Search

I was born Mary Katherine Maurer and raised as Katherine Anne Linn in a wonderful city in the Midwest where people were considerate of others, had a great work ethic, and the public education system was outstanding. In my opinion, Des Moines, the capital city of Iowa, was an idyllic place to grow up. I was born there because my birth mother needed a place to hide out and work while she was pregnant with me. As backward as that may sound today, "hiding out" was exactly what she was doing.

My birth mother was from a small town in Illinois where everyone knew each other, as well as all of their supposed secrets. Remaining in Clinton once her pregnancy was physically obvious would have had the gossip mill blowing up like an active volcano. She was twenty-three, unmarried, and her boyfriend, my birth father, vacillated in his support of them bringing a baby into the world. She told her two sisters that she was pregnant but never told her parents or her brother. Eventually her younger sister, Rita, would share this secret with Rita's only daughter, Jill. If Rita had not shared this secret with her youngest child, I most likely never would have had the opportunity to meet my sister and tell this story.

My birth mother grew up in the late 1930s through the 1950s in a large, strict Catholic family. Telling her parents that she was with child out of wedlock in 1959 would have been unbearable for her, primarily because she felt that her mom and dad would be extremely disappointed in her. Whether this was an overreaction on my birth mother's part or a fairly accurate assessment we will never know. She moved to and remained in Des Moines for the last four months of her pregnancy and then delivered in the same hospital where she had been working in labor and delivery as a nurse. Three months after my birth, she was off to a new job and a new life in Denver, along with a few of her dear nursing buddies. I was placed in the hands of Catholic Charities of Des Moines, where the social workers did a bang-up job of matching me with my adoptive parents.

Mom and Dad (which is how I will refer to my adoptive parents throughout the remainder of this book) were kind and loving people who had been hoping to adopt a child for almost four-and-a-half years. They were political moderates; Dad was raised in a somewhat religious Presbyterian household and Mom in a very religious Catholic family. Dad was an only child and Mom was the youngest of six children. Both were from close families and were probably everything on my birth mother's checklist for the perfect placement. As I've expressed for most of my life (ever since I was old enough to realize it), I won the adoption lottery.

While growing up, my observations about adopted children were pretty narrow-minded. From the limited number of friends that I had who were also adopted, experience showed me that if children were not happy with their adoptive parents or their family life in general, they would be more likely to seek their birth mothers and/or birth fathers, as well as possible siblings. It seemed to me that it was simply a defense mechanism to discover the happy family life that they dreamed of if the first round with their adoptive family hadn't worked out so well. This was my myopic view of adoption as a child growing up with adoptive parents. Closed minded? Yes. Based on limited experience? Absolutely.

Growing up, I never really thought that searching for birth parents was any more convoluted than that.

You're unhappy? You searched for your birth relatives. Happy? No need to search. I had one sibling that I grew up with, my brother Jamie. He was also adopted at birth, a little less than four years after me. I don't recall us ever discussing the possibility of searching for birth parents when we were kids. We had two different sets of biological parents, so potentially the discoveries of these two mothers and two fathers could have had wildly different outcomes. I wonder now . . . was the curiosity there when we were children, or was that too much for a kid to wrap their head around?

I discovered later that my limited exposure to other adoptees and their family situations didn't give me an even remotely accurate picture of the complexities involved. As time evolved, so did my opportunity to meet more adoptees, all with varying experiences. The decision to search for a birth mother or birth father can have an almost unlimited number of catalysts. I also learned from those who have observed and worked on cases for years that adoptees have also chosen to *not* pursue any information when they've had a tough family life with their adoptive parents or family. Adoptees who have experienced a wonderful, loving upbringing may also choose to search for a birth parent for a myriad of reasons. These decisions are all very personal and unique.

As I also discovered at a very young age, just simply being adopted can have its social challenges. It wasn't just about your inner thoughts and feelings surrounding this thing that made you different from most of your peers. There was the added element of some children wanting to express their opinion about you being different from them. Specifically, you not being the biological child of the parents who were raising you.

※ ※ ※

It was 1966, and a nice summer day to be outside in Des Moines. My parents had built a house back in 1960, shortly after I was born, to accommodate their expanding family. The best thing about the location was that it was on a dead-end street with only four houses, and our house was the last one on the left. A deep creek, usually dry, ran all the way along the opposite side of the street from the four houses. This setup, along with the wonderful sledding hill that ran along the side and back of our yard, made our little neighborhood the perfect place for all of us neighbor kids to hang out and play together— sometimes all day on the weekends and during summers. We all had different dinner bells that our parents would ring when it was time to come inside for supper. We were allowed to play outside for several hours, as long as we made sure to come quickly when our bell rang.

Being that it was one of those beautiful summer days, my next-door neighbor, Fred, and I were enjoying our usual activities: systematically trolling the creek for critters; playing four-square in the street in front of my house; and swinging on the swing set in his backyard. Of all our neighbors, Fred and I were the closest in age, about a year apart. I suppose that is why we spent so much time together and we got along so famously. However, as that afternoon went on, some sort of disagreement developed while we were taking turns sliding down the slide. Fred had known since an early age that I was adopted, but had never said anything cruel about it, as kids tend to do when someone is different from them in any way. For whatever reason, though, that changed on that afternoon. Once we got into it, Fred turned to me and said, "You're an orphan."

Needless to say, as a six-year-old, this was about the worst thing anyone could throw at me. I can still hear the malice in his voice as if it were yesterday. My parents had told me ever since I was old enough to comprehend that my brother and I were adopted, but no one had ever said that I was an orphan. I burst into tears and went running into my house, where I saw my dad as soon as I walked in. He saw how distraught I was and immediately wrapped those long, loving arms of his around me as he always did so well. He asked me what was wrong, and I told him what Fred had just called me. My dad, always quick on his feet, didn't even miss a beat. He walked me over to the den, where several shelves of books included our big family dictionary. He let me know that together we were going to look up the definition of the word *orphan*. I was still crying as we flipped through the pages. He got us to the right page, and he said, "Hmmm . . . it says here that an orphan is someone who has no parents. That hardly seems to be your situation, young lady. As I see it, technically you have four parents: your mom and me, plus two birth parents. That's a whole lot more than most children have!"

Classic Chuck Linn. He was always there to prop me up and that day was no different. On a moment's notice, he thought to shed light on the meaning of that word used as a nasty insult to make me realize that I was far from an orphan and actually a very lucky young lady. The way in which he chose to approach this once again showed that my dad was and had always been my mighty protector.

Fast forward several decades. It was late spring of 2012, and I was fifty-two years old, married, and had three children. It was late at night and everyone in my house was asleep but me. I was sitting at my computer, my thoughts drifting far away from the task in front of me. I found myself staring out the window into our very dark, quiet front yard and suddenly the thought came to me . . . our precious three daughters were approaching or had already arrived at early adulthood, and they only had exposure to 50 percent of their medical history and backgrounds.

This thought drifted into my head seemingly out of nowhere, but by that point in my life I knew that ideas that "come out of nowhere" tend to have a distinct purpose. I have come to learn over the years that this is my strongest form of communication with my guides or, as some prefer to call them, guardian angels. I was getting a very strong nudge to request a social and medical search for the health and well-being of our three children. Why it came to me when it did was a mystery at the time. As I realized just months afterward, this prompt had little to do with what minimal information on health history was available and a lot more to do with finding a very important person missing in my life.

Our daughters were no longer little girls. Lauren was already twenty-four years old, Carolyn was twenty-one, and Kat was zeroing in on adulthood at eighteen. Right then and there, I felt that it was time to put the wheels in motion to get some information for them. All I knew was that I was adopted from the Catholic Adoption Agency in Des Moines. I immediately did a search and found the phone number and address for Catholic Charities there, the organization that houses adoption services. I sat there staring at the address. I found it so odd that the place that had safeguarded so much private information about the beginning of my life was less than a ten-minute drive from our house in Des Moines and I never knew it.

The Christ Child Home, one of the chief buildings used by Catholic Charities, was the beautiful old home where I was kept as soon as my birth mother relinquished her legal rights to me. Here, all children up for adoption with Catholic Charities in Des Moines were housed and cared for until placed with their adoptive parents. That home was even closer, only a few minutes' drive from our old house on Arapahoe. I thought about how there were literally hundreds of times growing up that my mom drove both my brother and me by these two places, back and forth on the main street by our neighborhood. Unbeknownst to me until I began conducting research that night, these two buildings both sat on Grand Avenue, twenty-three blocks from each other. Did my mom ever glance over at each place as we spurred on, thinking about how this is where our little family began, while my brother and I played in the back seat, innocent and unaware?

An adoptee that is seeking information from the adoption agency has a couple of search methods. The first is to elect to search for your birth mother and/or birth father. This could potentially lead to finding out about siblings and all sorts of other relatives. The other choice is to do a social/medical search, which allows you to be privy to whatever information was left on the adoption forms filled out by the birth mother and possibly the birth father. This search provides general social information about the birth parents, and, occasionally, details about their families. Examples of social information that might be disclosed would be physical descriptions of each parent, like eye color, hair color, complexion, and height. Other social details could include religious preferences, family backgrounds, and even their occupations or family businesses. This latter search is conducted with very little personal information available in the records about the birth parents.

My knowledge of what to expect in a social/medical search was based on searches other adoptees had shared with me and the expectations laid out for me by the social worker at Catholic Charities. In this less invasive search, the agency keeps it vague on purpose. The information released is much less detailed in this type of search. For example, sharing the birth mother's first name and last initial—same for the birth father—seems to be standard protocol for the social/medical search. Information about where birth parents grew up is usually limited to the state, not the city or town—for example, John D. of Maryland and Jane D. of Indiana. Any major health issues through each of their bloodlines (if the father's is reported, you're lucky) is usually rather limited, but every bit is obviously helpful.

Once again, even that information in this type of search tends to be vague while somewhat informative; things like "maternal grandfather died of a heart attack at age seventy-three," as opposed to more specific medical information such as the blood types of the birth parents. I already knew before contacting Catholic Charities that it was the social and medical search that I wanted to request, because I was hoping to obtain some of the medical background that our daughters were lacking. Although going into it I had no idea what medical information I would receive, anything was better than what I had before, which was nothing!

It made me think back to decades ago, when one of my best friends, Cile, had requested this type of search. She did not want any identifying information, but still got an enormous amount of social and medical history. As I learned, there is no guarantee regarding the amount of details that might have been provided by the birth mother; you just hope and pray that it will be enough to provide your progeny with some background that will be useful for them. I recall Cile reading pages upon pages of information to me when she received her report. Fortunately for Cile, her record had a substantive amount of both medical and social information.

I suspect that there is not a standard questionnaire that is filled out by birth mothers anywhere and everywhere when they are giving up a child for adoption. Although the questions most likely have a lot of consistency, I believe that the greater difference from one survey to the next has more to do with the willingness of the birth mother to share information. I believe that my friend Cile got very lucky and had an extremely long-winded birth mother that felt compelled to leave as much information as she could. To me, it was a profound revelation going into a process like this and having no set record of the beginning of my life. What you discover or what is missing could easily depend on who filled out the forms about you and your biological relatives!

The next morning, I contacted the agency to discuss my desire to conduct a social/medical search. Their process fascinated me; they asked me a series of questions, which were directly related to which type of search is chosen. Since the social/medical search is much less invasive than the birth parent search, it didn't take long to ask me the questions and get things rolling. I did find out that birth parents can opt out of having their names or any of their personal information in the file be revealed. A biological parent may submit this desire any time between when the child is born and when the formal request is made by the adoptee. Thus, I already had my guard up just in case I was not going to be allowed to obtain even a first name of my biological mother or father.

They located my file almost immediately and I gladly paid my fee. Upon hanging up the phone I realized how excited I was to get this information. My level of heightened anticipation actually caught me off guard. It occurred to me that not only did I want to get whatever medical history I could for the girls, but now I abruptly realized that this woman who gave me up for adoption was a living, breathing human being. I'd never really been asked what my expectations were regarding my birth parents, so when asked any questions at all about my thoughts about them, I was somewhat stunned. Maybe I'd dwelled on it less than some might, but up until that point they had no physical description in my mind. They were both just "blobs" out there in space. They didn't have a face, height, hair color, eye color, or any other distinguishing characteristic that might have been conjured up in my mind over time. I had plenty of opportunities to wonder where I got certain physical characteristics—athleticism, love of learning, love of anything artistic . . . really anything that made me "me"—but I had never formulated a picture in my mind of what either one of them looked like. Whether or not this was a psychological protective mechanism on my part or just a lack of interest due to my deep love for the parents who raised me I honestly cannot answer. I do acknowledge that it is certainly very plausible to love your adoptive parents with all of your soul and still wonder about your genetic makeup.

At the end of my conversation with the social worker, she guessed that the packet of information would be completed sometime within the next few days and that I would receive it in the mail in a week or more. I put this timeline in the back of my mind and moved on to my other projects. To my delight, the envelope arrived in our mailbox five days later. I took my usual walk down the drive to our mailbox, opened it to retrieve the mail, and saw *the envelope*. As I pulled it out, I was surprised that the package was rather full. Not huge—but just thicker than I had expected it to be. My calm suddenly slipped into exhilaration, complete with my heart pounding out of my chest and my palms slick with sweat. I walked (no, ran) into our house and went straight to the couch in the living room to open the envelope and soak up this information about the beginning of my life, which had all been stowed away under lock and key for fifty-two years.

The first few pages just verified the adoption, my given name, and the names of my birth parents . . . and they actually had *names*, they weren't just blobs after all! Margaret M.! Robert S.! This was becoming more intriguing to me by the second.

The report was basically an outline prepared by the adoption case manager. The information first discussed my name given at birth (Mary Katherine), which was where I first had to stop and take a deep breath. What were the chances that both my birth mother and adoptive mother had named me Katherine? My parents had named me Katherine, after my adoptive maternal grandmother, and Anne, after my adoptive paternal grandmother. Where did Katherine come from in my birth mother's mind? Was this just a coincidence? I seriously doubted it. Next, I read about when and where I was born (Des Moines, Iowa), birth statistics, and health condition of both the baby and mother (excellent).

The next two sections outlined personal information regarding each birth parent, keeping it non-identifying in nature. As this was a social/medical search rather than a search for my birth parents, I was excited to see information that I didn't even know if I would receive: their years of birth, their religions, and their physical descriptions. I noted that at six feet tall, I was the exact midpoint in height between the two, and that my green eyes could have come from either one of them. The report also detailed their education levels and occupations.

The last page outlined the social and medical history as communicated by my birth mother, including their dating for six months and the decision to move away when she discovered that she was pregnant. The document explored her time in Des Moines, as well as my birth and her release of custody. She also laid out some of her family's medical history, but there really wasn't that much. In my eyes, that was a good thing as an adoptee. The last thing you want to see in a medical history report is a long line of serious illnesses or early deaths that you've just discovered is in your bloodline, especially five decades into your life! At the end of the outline, it mentioned that she wrote on and off to the social worker involved in her case for about a year after my birth.

Imagine my surprise when I turned to the next page and witnessed my birth mother's handwriting for the first time in my life! Attached to the document were three additional pages: photocopies of handwritten letters from Margaret to her social worker on the case. I immediately noticed how eerily similar my cursive was to hers at the same age. It was fascinating to me to read these letters, which I perused over and over before setting them aside. It was the first insight into my birth mother as a real person. Even though there were just two notes, I was able to get a feel for her kind heart and loving personality. I stared at them, amazed that the current social worker had thought to make copies of these handwritten letters, giving me the opportunity to witness my birth mother's script. Years later, another worker at the same agency mentioned to me how odd it was that the original employee who had put my packet together had added those copies of the handwritten notes. She stated that that was not part of standard protocol.

The last documents in my packet were copies of hand-typed (I mean the *real* old-fashioned type—straight from an old-fashioned typewriter—that was commonly used in the '50s and '60s) letters of "application." The adoption agency had requested that prospective adoptive parents write autobiographical notes explaining why they would make good parents. The first one was from my dad, the second was from my mom. I had never seen these letters. As I held the copies in front of me, I wondered why they had never shared them with me. Imagine condensing your wish of this level of intensity down to two to five pages. It seemed unfathomable to me. Their words stirred an immense love in my heart; I could palpably feel the intense yearning they had for a child of their own.

Both letters followed a similar format. First came their personal background—where they were born and when, their parents, education, occupations, and information that might shed light on why they would be the best parents for their prospective adopted child. My mother emphasized the Catholic faith that ran deep in her side of the family, as this application was being submitted to an institution of that same denomination. I also got a chuckle out of one of my dad's last statements regarding his recent admittance as a junior member to Wakonda, the most prestigious country club in Des Moines. Looking back on it was amusing, as if he was saying, "Look at us! We can provide our child with a nice upbringing!" I'm not sure that I would have found that to be appropriate if I were in his shoes, but I got it. They were going to tell the adoption agency anything that might shed even the tiniest bit of light on how they could care for and be good parents to their adopted child. It spoke to me about how long they had painfully waited for a child of their own.

More than anything, I was shocked that there were copies of these priceless applications from my parents in my file. I had no idea that they had been asked to write their stories as part of the adoption application process; this had never come up in conversation between Mom, Dad, and me. Jamie had never mentioned it either, and I felt sure he would have told me if he had ever heard about them or seen them. To be able to have insight into their thoughts at that pivotal time, not just their personal memoirs, was an exquisitely special gift to me.

And the mention of "Wakonda" in Dad's application was a nod to the future. I spent so many wonderful years growing up there. Swimming was a big part of my life for many years; I learned how to swim at four years old right there in that pool in "Clark's Corner," and kept on swimming up to and in college. The amazing Clark Munger donned a white pith helmet every day in the same corner of the pool, where there was enough shade to teach young children how to swim. Many of those three-, four-, and five-year-old students of his went on to be very successful competitive swimmers. Clark and his signature hat were a staple at Wakonda for years.

My parents spent as much time there on the golf course as my brother and I did in the pool. To this day, when I walk out my front door in Nashville and hear the "chink" of a golfer teeing off on the golf course next to our little cul-de-sac, I smile and think of hearing that sound when I was coming up for air in the Wakonda pool and seeing my dad clicking along in his golf shoes, directing his immense smile back at me.

Years later, in the spring of 2016 after my mom Ruth Ann passed, my husband Don and I were cleaning out

Mom and Dad's house. I found the originals of their hand-typed biographies in one of my dad's "manila folder files." This was a term that I endearingly gave to my father's storage habit of putting everything that ever happened in our family's lives into a manila folder, with a very specific headline on the upper tab in his distinct handwriting with its backward slant. There were files with copies of life insurance premiums paid, cars bought and sold, receipts for artwork purchased, house blueprints, you name it.

On top of the usual files that you would expect to find were Dad's meticulously labeled records for minutiae such as "Kathe's first grade report cards," "Jamie—kindergarten art," or "500-yard freestyle splits—high school." There were so many hundreds of files that it was no wonder I had never run into those precious originals of their autobiographies when Mom had asked me to help her find documents in the years after Dad's death and before she passed herself. The vast majority of the files needed to be recycled or shredded, which caused me to almost overlook the autobiographies and throw them into the recycling bin. I now had their original hand-typed letters!

Letter e1 to Catholic Charities

Autobiography by Charles G. Linn

July 15, 1958

I, Charles G. Linn, came into this world just in time for dinner at 6 p.m. on the 9th day of August 1928. The town was Grand Island, Nebr. with the St. Francis Catholic Hospital serving as host. Dad was very proud of Mom and me since we didn't keep the doctor from his dinner.

From my baby pictures I looked quite healthy, and whenever the slightest sniffle occurred, I am sure Dad would rush me to the Grand Island Clinic for observation where he worked in the medical profession as a practicing Eye, Ear, Nose & Throat Specialist until 1929 when we moved to the South Bend Clinic, South Bend, Indiana. I soon decided that this town was much too large & high powered for my early years, and in 1931 I talked the folks into moving 26 miles west to a little town called La Porte, Indiana. A county seat town with a friendly smile, sporting some 16,000 neighbors, where a fella could walk down the street and be called by his first name.

We moved into a modest house on the main avenue in town and my first recollection seems to be looking up and down the street at the hundreds of beautiful maple trees. (La Porte is nicknamed The Maple City.) Just knowing that this was where I wanted to learn what everything was all about.

And learn I did. My first black eye was delivered by the boy next door when I was 4. He thought I was some kind of foreigner when I told him my dad had Scotch-Irish and English blood in him while Mother (maiden name "Lichty") had German with a drop of Scotch & a lot of English in her. When I convinced him that this all added up to American, we became fast friends and spent the next 12 years just being boys.

I had to depend on friends as playmates & companions when Dad & Mom weren't around since I was destined to be an only child. Now many children seem to resent being an only child, but I wouldn't have traded my parents for all of the brothers and sisters in the world. This still goes today, and if given one child or a dozen to raise, I only hope that I can pass on most of the fine ingredients which my parents offered me.

I started to kindergarten at age 5 & went on through 5th grade in the same old school building called Lincoln. I'm sure that I enjoyed recess more than "book learning" but was mighty proud when I graduated from 5th grade & moved next door to Junior High.

It was there that I took my first dancing lesson, played on the basketball team as center, fell quietly in love with my Social Science teacher and flunked my first & only class in woodworking. The teacher said I was all thumbs & couldn't build a birdhouse, and you know something, I still can't.

At age twelve the folks could see where some strong outside discipline was needed. We had just moved into a large, old house on the edge of town with a three-acre lawn and I immediately set the garage on fire while trying to light a cigarette, both of which made me deathly ill. My punishment was being sent to Culver Military School where a young fellow gets molded into a fine figure of a man & loves every minute of it. I spent four summers at this school and managed to graduate with honors.

I entered high school as an average student with a good deal of awe & admiration for those upper classmen. My studies were secondary during those four years, and I think my only regret upon graduating in 1945 was that I hadn't given myself fully to studying & had graduated no better than the top 3rd of my class. I managed to let-ter in golf & tennis, worked on the school yearbook for 2 years, played a small part in school politics and I'm sure enjoyed my senior year with as much vigor as any young man preparing for college & yet not really thinking too seriously about it. I met my wife while still a junior in High School and she helped celebrate my graduation by favoring me at the Senior Prom.

The next year found me heading for DePauw University. My stay there was short lived since I had become very unsettled in my thinking and couldn't adjust myself to the thought of taking on a major study course & sticking with it. Thus, after a year of indecision, I dropped out of De Pauw and went to work in a factory in La Porte doing assembly work on a production line. It was probably the most unproductive year of my life, but I'm sure it helped build in me a better understanding and maturity when it came to facing the tough environment outside of my parents' front door.

In the fall of 1949, I headed due west for school with Simpson College, located in Indianola, Iowa as my goal. This school seemed to fit my needs beautifully & I settled down to the work of mastering the Business Administration major which I had elected. The Alpha Tau Omega fraternity pledged me the same year and I still find myself engaged in various types of work for that fraternity even today. My future wife joined me at this school the following year where we remained until the 12th day of February 1951.

The Korean conflict was boiling & I found myself inducted into the army. My two years were spent state side in Camp Rucker, Alabama & the two schools the Army sent me to. One offered me 4 months of training in meteorology at Fort Sill, Oklahoma, while the other gave me 5 months of training at leadership school in

Camp Chaffee, Ark. Both schools helped straighten my backbone and I must brag about graduating at the head of my class (out of 300 students) in leadership school. After finishing these two courses I wound up my career in the army pounding a typewriter (of all things) for the Commanding General of the 47th Division in charge of Artillery.

My honorable discharge in February of 1953 left the doors open for a job with the Gilcrest Lumber Company which I took and have been with them for the past 5 years. My apprenticeship with the company was a back breaking year of work in the yard unloading box cars and trying to learn what a 2x4 looked like. This hard work seemed to wear down my male independence and I suddenly found myself happily married to my high school & college sweetheart on Sept. 5, 1953. We honeymooned in New Orleans & took up residence in the Joan Apartments located at 2925 Grand Ave, Des Moines, IA.

I went back to my training at Gilcrest Lumber while my wife found a secretarial job with Holmes Oldsmobile where she worked for two years. In 1956 my wife's savings helped place a down payment on the house we are now living in & she left her job for the more demanding duties of a busy housewife.

In 1957 I was honored with the Vice Presidency & Treasurer's job at Gilcrest Lumber and was accepted as a member at The Wakonda Club. More recently I have been taken into membership at The Des Moines Club.

Now that I am approaching 30 years of age, and have just written my first autobiography, I must look back & be thankful for what I have been given. I have no desire to relive these first years of my life since what lies ahead can only add to the pleasures & blessed memories in my past. I have nothing to hide & only hope that I can give to my future children all, if not more of, the rich & bountiful gifts which my parents, church & friends have given me.

Letter #2 to Catholic Charities

Autobiography of Ruth Ann Pelz Linn

July 15, 1958

On June 23, 1930, I, Ruth Ann Pelz Linn, was born to William and Katherine Pelz at the Holy Family Hospital in LaPorte, Indiana. My most vivid memories are those of being raised in a big family. I have 5 older brothers and sisters. Juanita, Katherine, Bill, Jim, Louie, and I am the youngest. Our home was large and so was the property surrounding.

You might say to fit the needs. We didn't have a farm but a large acreage on the outskirts of town, 9 acres of which was an apple orchard.

During the summer months, most of the activity centered on helping our parents in the orchard. It was quite a busy family project and business. This was in addition to a Sporting Goods and Auto Supply Store my father owned in town.

When I started grade school at St. Joseph's Catholic School, my parents moved me to the city to live with my aunt and uncle, Mr. & Mrs. Louis Borgerd. Since they had no children of their own, all six of us would take turns living with them. (It sometimes was a battle royale waiting for our turns.) I enjoyed it tremendously since playmates in the country were few and far between and suddenly, I had many new friends. I have never known why but I lived with them until I started high school at La Porte High.

During Grade School I enjoyed many and various activities. I really was a tom boy at heart but they would never allow me on the football field, so second best I was a cheerleader. I sang in the school choir for 5 years, helped the nuns clean the altar and sanctuary and at one time read the Mass aloud in English while the priest was saying Mass. I also participated in and loved the many Easter and May Day processions.

High School was a big busy 4 years. School books and studies seemed so incidental at the time. Club activities, football games, basketball games, formals and social life were the one and only concern. In fact, in the midst of this, I met my husband Charles and the last 2 years of high school we dated quite regularly.

After graduation I decided to work a year before entering college. I certainly am glad I did because I settled down quite a bit in that year. So in the fall of '49 I entered Simpson College, Indianola, Iowa. I stayed there until February of '51 and then transferred to The South Bend College of Commerce, South Bend, Indiana where I took a secretarial training course for 6 months. At the end of this time, I was offered a position at the Indiana State Highway Commission where I remained until my marriage to Charles Linn, September 5, 1953.

He instantly brought me to Des Moines, and we moved into an apartment at 2925 Grand Ave. After a few months, I took a position with Holmes Oldsmobile Co. for 2 years during which time we started construction on our new home and present address, 2805 Gilmore. We have lived there for 2 ½ years.

I believe I have considered adoption for nearly three years. Because of a serious illness in 1952 and the result of many operations, the doctors have never been too hopeful that I could or would have a child. I do believe that a child or children are a blessing from God. We do know whatever happens to us as individuals are His intentions for us. But if it be the case that I cannot bear my own child, that He will see fit to give us a child by means of caring for someone else's child.

❀ ❀ ❀

Once I had culled my parents' letters, I went back to focus on the copies of the handwritten letters to the social worker from my birth mother. She was very forthright in her letters, thanking the social worker immensely for getting her through the birth and adoption process so smoothly without her parents finding out anything. As you may recall at the beginning of my story, Margaret had moved to Des Moines for the last part of her pregnancy with me, before her parents could tell that she was "expecting." In this file newly placed in my hands, I now had a bit more important information—she was employed as a gynecologic/obstetric nurse at Mercy Hospital in Des Moines until my birth. This sent a ping of recognition in my head . . . one of my two best friends growing up was Liz Moore. Her dad was a highly respected gynecologist and obstetrician in Des Moines for decades. He practiced primarily out of Iowa Methodist Hospital but also had privileges at Mercy Hospital. It suddenly occurred to me

55

that since Margaret had worked at Mercy Gynecology and Obstetrics from May through September 1959 as a pregnant, unwed mother, it would be highly unlikely for Dr. Moore or anyone else working there not to have noticed her. There was the possibility that they may have worked together on occasion, but that of course is just my speculation.

Then I remembered something even more interesting. I recalled my mom, Ruth Ann, telling me something a few years before she passed on. Dick Moore, Liz's father, had been her gynecologist during Mom and Dad's early days in Des Moines, back when she was having fertility issues and could not become pregnant. I don't recall why we even got on the topic, but I remember thinking when my mom told me this that it was so odd that I had never heard this before, especially with Liz and I being dear friends for decades. There is the possibility that my mom had mentioned this many, many years back and maybe it didn't stick with me. After all, Liz and I met in first grade dance class, so even if Mom had told me, "Oh yes, her dad is my doctor!" I doubt I would recall. I have a very good memory, but that was half a lifetime ago!

Of course, I couldn't wait to call Liz to tell her this story and see if she'd ever heard anything about the connection between my parents adopting me and the possibility of her dad working with Margaret. She knew nothing about it, but honestly I didn't expect her to. Sadly, Dr. Moore had passed two years previous to that, so I didn't have the opportunity to ask him.

Whether my birth mother and Dr. Moore met during the same period that he was my mom's gynecologist is a question that will never be answered. However, it was beginning to seem like there were possible correlations that I could no longer ignore. In a short time, I had gone from seeing my birth mother as an indescribable blob out in space to being exceedingly curious about every little detail. My head was grappling with the ever-changing information and finding a way to process it. This was yet another example of how I learned pretty quickly through this process that sometimes you run into little victories in the search and other times you run into dead ends. Regardless, pieces of the puzzle were starting to come together.

Back to my file, sitting in my lap. In one of her handwritten letters, Margaret went on to explain that in December after my birth, she and a few of her best friends from nursing school took positions at a medical center in Colorado. The name of the medical center was whited out in her letter, but it was fairly simple for me to look up the names of hospitals, logically starting with those in the Denver area. It had to be a pretty sizable institution to be able to offer a position to all three nurses moving together at the same time. Based also on the length of the name whited out, I deduced that they likely had all gone to work at University of Colorado Medical Center. As I mentioned previously, most identifiers are eliminated when an adoptee asks for just a social/medical record. This was the case with where my biological mother moved in Colorado; neither thname of the city nor the medical center were left legible on the copies sent to me.

After thoroughly combing through this fascinating insight into my birth mother, I was completely shocked to see that the social worker had accidentally forgotten to white out my *birth mother's last name* where she signed the letter. I *could not believe* what I was seeing. This type of mistake is just not supposed to happen on a social/medical search report!

Within an instant, my whole perspective on this process changed. The adrenaline rush that I experienced in that moment caused my entire body to react . . . my chest felt tight and my hands shook uncontrollably. I was utterly shocked at how strong both my physical and mental reactions to this unexpected bombshell were. Something that just days ago I thought I had no

Copies of Margaret's handwritten letters.

interest in became a lofty obsession in a mere moment. I had switched gears from thinking I just wanted medical background for my children to wanting to do everything I could to find out my birth mother's married last name, if she had married and taken a new last name, and whether she was still living.

My immediate reaction to this exposed last name—albeit her maiden name—made me jump up from our living room couch and run over to the den to start searching on our computer for her, seeking out possible marriage announcements, obituaries, and the like. The next afternoon, I called Catholic Charities to talk to the adoption case manager who had researched my file and sent my report. I found out that within the time that she had mailed my file and when I had received it, she had stopped working for Catholic Charities. I had been assigned a new case manager named Kim Laube. Although I didn't know it at the time, not only was my original social worker's *accidentally* leaving my birth mother's last name on the handwritten letters a "God wink," but having Kim as my new case manager was another divine gift as well.

I became an amateur detective, searching in the oddest places and then making certain assumptions to go down one path. If that turned into a dead end, then I would back up to the point where I was pretty sure the prior information had all been accurate and then go down another path. I found it interesting that when I charted these paths with my handwritten notes it looked like a tree—a family tree! This went on for days on end. I would carve out hours during the day as well as at night when there wasn't something else I was obligated to be doing. I was truly enjoying the challenge of figuring out who she was on my own accord, until it seemed like my push forward became the equivalent of a train that had run out of steam. Eventually I ran into some pretty big hurdles, because early information about her, including any wedding announcements in newspapers, occurred prior to all written information anywhere being plastered all over the internet as it is these days.

My efforts were becoming futile when my three daughters, Lauren, Carolyn, and Kat, must have picked up on how much my view of this search had changed. I now was just as interested in finding out who my birth mother was as I was previously only interested in finding out about our medical backgrounds. They announced to me around a week before Mother's Day 2012 that they were giving me a birth mother search in honor of that holiday. It brought me to tears on and off for several days—such a thoughtful gift from three girls whose lives would have never commenced had it not been for the selfless act of one woman.

New thoughts began racing through my head with the current direction that this hunt had taken . . . was my birth mother still alive? If so, where did she live? Where she grew up or somewhere thousands of miles away? How would she react to being contacted after over fifty years? Lauren, my oldest daughter, contacted our new social worker, Kim, at Catholic Charities to instigate the search. Next came another questionnaire that I filled out, based on this new search. I did answer that I was only interested in finding my birth mother, not other biological relatives, such as half brothers, sisters, or father. I expressed that I already had a family, that I loved my parents and my brother dearly, and that I wasn't looking for another tribe. I think back to those answers now and realize how my thoughts and feelings about these searches clearly evolved over time. Just because I have a family that I love doesn't necessarily mean I can't establish other connections, especially those that are biological. This didn't mean a new family . . . it meant shared connections.

Now that I had answered these questions for my birth mother search, the next step was to hurry up and wait. Time sure moves slowly when you have committed to taking the plunge!

CHAPTER 3

A Series of Fortunate Events

About three weeks after Lauren requested the birth mother search, I met my daughter for lunch near her office outside of downtown Nashville. It was a stunning summer day in 2012, with the bluest of skies and a great temperature. We met at our usual lunch dive, both ordered and enjoyed our favorite salads, and then said goodbye to head off to the rest of our busy days. I got to my car in the parking lot, unlocked it, and climbed in.

Before I'd even turned on the ignition, my cell phone began singing to me, and I saw that it was Kim Laube.

My heart started racing. I hesitated to pick up, because I was about to get either extremely good news or very poignant news of an opportunity missed by not acting sooner. Once again, I found myself in an emotional situation where my reactions to anything to do with biological family were 180 degrees away from what they'd been for the vast majority of my life. The fact that I had such a strong physical and emotional reaction to simply seeing Kim's name show up on my cell told me volumes about how important this hunt for my birth mother had become. I had now had about three weeks to stew over the possibility of actually finding my birth mother, which was new territory for my previously rather closed mind.

I picked up the phone and said hello to Kim. She immediately got to the point.

"Hi Kathe, are you in the middle of something?"

"No, Kim . . . this is great timing."

"I have found out some information for you. There is both good news and bad news. Which would you like to hear first?"

I set down my keys and braced myself. I felt sure that I knew what the bad news was. Kim would not have been calling just to tell me that she hadn't gotten anywhere in finding my birth mother. Kim was too busy *and* too organized to be making calls like that. I spat out my choice. "The bad news, please."

"I found out who your birth mother is, and you were definitely on the right track. However, I'm sorry to tell you that she passed about nine-and-a-half years ago."

Although I remember Kim's most compassionate delivery of this new disclosure, I don't even remember how I responded. Realistically, I had known ever since I had first held that file in my hands from Catholic Charities that there was a distinct possibility that my birth mother had already passed. I had no regrets for not having her as the mother who raised me. Although I know now that Margaret was an incredible human being and mother, she made the right choice at a time when she couldn't raise a child alone. My "real" mother was the woman who raised me—Ruth Ann Linn.

To this day, when I have conversations with friends or acquaintances about my being adopted, it always surprises me when someone refers to my birth parents as my "real" parents! The context, almost every time it's been discussed, is usually of the following nature: "Okay, so these are your adoptive parents . . . did you ever find out who your *real* parents are?" I reiterated to myself at that moment what I knew was true in my heart. Margaret did the right and noble thing by giving me up for adoption because her situation would not have provided adequately for a child.

From the moment that my daughters instigated my birth mother search, I knew there was one primary reason that I felt strongly about communicating with my long-lost biological mother. I simply wanted to have the opportunity to thank her deeply for going through all that she did to have me and let her know that she made the perfect choice in placing me with my parents. I also had come to the realization that I had always loved her, just not in the traditional sense of a daughter's love for her mother. There was and still is a deep respect for all that she did for me under great duress. For most of my life, she was a complete unknown to me, with the exception of what she had done for me. Without her, I would never have enjoyed the love of my parents, my brother, my grandparents, my husband, my children, and all of the other people in my life that I hold so dearly in that precious compartment in the center of my heart.

From the research I had done to this point, I knew wholeheartedly that many young women who had given up their babies for adoption in the 1950s and '60s did so because they were forced to do so by their own parents (or adult relatives sworn to secrecy), their teachers, nuns, or priests. It had so much to do with the stigma of that time period—in the culture of white America, you simply did not raise a child out of wedlock as a single mother. Thinking about this in today's culture, this social mindset seems almost peculiar. In the '50s and '60s, a young woman in her teens or early twenties would quietly disappear in the middle of the school year or for the summer under any one of a number of ruses made up by the adult or adults that were attempting to "save her reputation," when in reality: 1) there was no consideration for the emotional scars and consequences that the single mother would quietly try to suppress but would carry with her until the day she left this earth, and 2) oftentimes the adult or adults forcing the unwed mother to surrender her child were interested in saving face themselves, not wanting anyone to know that *their* daughter, niece, or student (insert the appropriate noun) was capable of such abominable behavior before having walked down the aisle and said "I do." The advice given to these poor girls usually went something like this: "The best thing you can do for yourself and this baby is to put your mistake behind you and forget about it."

Mistake. I think about that word *a lot*. Even nowadays, people use that ugly term when they are gossiping, talking about someone who got pregnant unexpectedly. Or much sooner than planned. Or how about that fourth or fifth baby that's born years after his or her older siblings? It's such an excruciatingly harsh word that completely dismisses the beauty of a baby coming into this world. That word in this context always makes me think of the dichotomy of the adoption process. On one side, you have a parent or parents that have waited through often considerable heartache attempting to conceive, who suddenly get the best news of their lives. A baby has been born and it is theirs to adopt, love, protect, raise, educate in faith and wisdom . . . and adore until he or she becomes an adult and maybe starts their own family someday.

On the polar side is oftentimes a single, unwed birth mother who, in most situations, is not getting the emotional support she needs in a time of crisis. Back in the 1950s and 1960s, she most likely had a considerable amount of pressure to surrender the baby for adoption, usually making the decision without the help of the birth father. He either denied even having had sex with her, or if he did acknowledge the possibility of being the father, wanted nothing to do with "settling down" by marrying, raising a child, and interrupting his life.

Obviously, there were also plenty of exceptions— young men who stood by their girlfriend and helped raise the child, married or unmarried. Clearly, we can never know the origin story of every adoption case, but in that time, in that era, quiet, secretive adoptions seemed to be the expected track for young, unwed women.

I thanked my middle daughter, Carolyn, profusely for putting the book *The Girls Who Went Away* by Ann Fessler in front of me shortly after the beginning of my search. She had read it in high school and suddenly realized it was probably a great resource for my quest.

That book would, in great detail, put my birth mother's and my situation into historical perspective.

Historical context is crucial with babies given up for adoption during that era. The period that I am referring to is post-World War II until the pivotal Roe v. Wade decision made by the U.S. Supreme Court in 1973. The Roe v. Wade verdict determined that a pregnant woman had the inherent right to decide whether to give birth to her unborn child or elect to have an abortion. This was key, along with the first oral contraceptive, Enovid, known widely as "The Pill," which was approved by the US Food and Drug Administration in 1960. Thus, I was born less than a year before oral contraception was made available to the American public and fourteen years before a federal mandate allowing pregnant women greater freedom in deciding whether or not to abort their unborn.

Looking at these dates often makes me realize how fortunate I am that I was born when I was. It used to bother me, once I was in my forties and older, that I wasn't born just months later, because being born in the next decade, the '60s, made one seem *much* younger than having a birth date in the end of 1959. Of course, once I realized how fortunate the timing of my birth was in relation to birth control and abortion legislation, I considered myself an extremely lucky person. Things were changing in the world of pregnancy and childbirth shortly after my birth and for the decades following. I have no idea what my birth mother would have done, had her pregnancy been at another time. Although I'm sure her decision was emotionally difficult, I'm thankful that I don't have to wonder.

When I was twenty-three years old, my mom, Ruth Ann, shared with me that she thought that my birth mother was much older than my birth father when I was born. She recalled, but wasn't sure, that my birth mother was thirty-seven and my birth father had been about twenty-six. Thus, when I found out almost three decades later that my birth mother was only twenty-four at the time that I was born, it became much more possible in my mind that she was still alive. It certainly would have meant a lot to me at that point to be able to simply thank her over the phone and emphasize that, in my mind, she had done the right thing back in 1959. As I had now missed the opportunity to speak to her, I could only hope that my deceased birth mother did not harbor guilt for the rest of her adult life over surrendering her baby. I wanted to take comfort in thinking that she knew it had worked out as it should, but now I would have to do some digging just to find out second- or third-hand.

When it comes to searching for a birth father, we'd assume it is usually pretty easy to track him down decades later because his last name wouldn't have changed. With a birth mother, the trick is discovering if she married, and how to go about finding her married name. If she has a very common last name, the hunt becomes that much more circuitous. While it's true nowadays that many women keep their surnames, many women also choose to change it or hyphenate. That was also true in the 1960s and 1970s, though perhaps not as common. She could have also changed her name for political or religious reasons, started going by a nickname, stopped using her given name . . . the possibilities of finding one single person across hand-typed documents from decades past is hard enough. Factoring in name changes makes the job seem daunting. It's tricky to know where to look beyond a name given at birth—and that's all I had.

In the summer of 2012, Kim, having vastly more experience in this arena than I did, set out looking for the names of all my birth mother's siblings. She fell upon some luck when she found the married last name of my birth mother's sister, who was two years her junior and was also the youngest of the siblings.

Kim discovered that my birth mother's youngest sister, Rita, and her husband, Duane, had married quite young and had lived at the same address in Clinton, Illinois for a very long time, raising their three children in that home. On the afternoon that Kim called the landline at that house hoping to speak to Rita, a bit of divine intervention again managed to slip its way into our sleuthing. Rita and Duane's youngest child, Jill, was walking into the house to check on her father, as she did faithfully. When the house phone rang, she answered.

Kim introduced herself as calling from Des Moines Catholic Charities. Jill immediately replied, "I know exactly why you're calling. My aunt gave up a baby daughter to your agency for adoption a long, long time ago and very few people knew about it. I'm one of them."

Less than one minute into the conversation, Kim was shocked and nearly speechless. As she recalled to me on the phone later that afternoon, she couldn't remember a time when she had made a call where she had identified herself as being with Catholic Charities and had the individual on the other end of the phone, someone not directly involved in the adoption, know exactly why she was calling. She of course was thrilled with this break in the case after weeks of searching for my birth mother's married name. When she asked Jill if her mother Rita was home, Jill sadly informed her that Rita had passed from complications of COPD almost three years before, in September 2009. Rita and Jill had been very close, so Rita had shared a lot with her daughter. Jill then went on to tell Kim my birth mother's full married name, as well as her nickname, Marti, and that unfortunately she had also passed, nine-and-a-half years ago. Jill was also able to provide Kim with a lot of information about the family tree. Having access to the names and married names of all of Marti's siblings and extended families, as well as her parents and grandparents, made it a whole new ball game for us. The great bonus news was that I had a new cousin out there—Jill!

Jill could not have been more helpful to Kim in recalling so much family information, including a rough idea of my birth father's last name. She did remember that his first name was Robert. She then handed Kim an even greater surprise, telling her that I had a sister, Marcia, who lived in Phoenix.

"I haven't talked to Marcia for some time but coincidentally, we just texted recently," Jill explained to Kim. "I will call her to tell her that you've called from Catholic Charities. I imagine that she'll be excited about this, but it's her decision if she wants to make contact with Kathe, and vice versa. Give me a day to get a hold of her and then maybe you can reach out to Marcia tomorrow?"

Having obtained this big breakthrough, Kim was excited to call me on that Friday summer afternoon, just as I had arrived at my car in the parking lot. Although she had to deliver the sad news about my birth mother's passing, she also had something very exciting to divulge. As I had not signed on for discovering identities of any biological relatives aside from my birth mother, my mind was wondering . . . what could the good news possibly be?

"Kathe, would you like to know the good news?"

"Yes, Kim. At this point I could use some more uplifting news."

"You have a younger sister. She lives in Arizona."

There was a long pause; the phone was silent for several seconds on both ends. I was lacking words and I felt as if my mouth was paralyzed. I think that Kim, being the extremely compassionate person that she is, was giving me time to absorb this revelation. She then went on to remind me about my answers to the questions that are part of every search procedure. In the survey that I had filled out from Catholic Charities, I had said that I was only interested in finding out who my birth mother was, and if still living, have the opportunity to reach out to her. Kim also pointed out that I had expressed an interest in not pursuing identities of any other biological relatives.

"Kathe, since you had expressed that you wanted the search to stop at finding Marti, we can halt right here.

Since it's Friday, why don't you take the weekend to sleep on it and decide whether or not you'd like to make contact with your sister? If you decide on Monday or Tuesday that you would like to approach her, there is a procedure we follow to make it as easy as possible for both parties."

Before Kim completed her sentence, I knew exactly how I felt. "Kim, I don't even need five minutes to change my mind. I've already decided. I definitely want to talk to her if she is open to it as well."

How did I do a complete turnaround regarding contacting a biological sibling? Not just a 180, but also on a moment's notice? These are the questions I ask myself when I look back on that day and think about the whole process. Who knows a person better than they know themselves? What would have happened and how would I have felt had that last name actually been whited out on my birth mother's two handwritten letters? Maybe it's not so clear-cut when dealing with matters of the heart.

Kim went on to explain how the process works. She would reach out to my sister to first see if she knew she had a female sibling, and then ask her if she would be open to meeting over the phone. If she was against the idea, then I would obviously need to respect that. If she was willing to talk, then Kim would email both of us with our respective contact information. I should then email my sister, introducing myself and asking if she would like to talk next week at a prearranged time so that we could both be alone for a while without distractions. Kim emphasized this point because she said this first call is usually very emotional and it would be best to not have any interruptions and have both parties able to give their full attention for a period of time. I eagerly agreed and then Kim went to work.

I was so excited to see what would happen. I realized that I might not hear anything back until the following week or later, as it was already late in the afternoon and Kim was reaching out by email first to ask if she could talk. By this point, I was probably about fifteen minutes from home, driving down the back streets from downtown Nashville instead of the highway because I was having trouble focusing after receiving this startling but very exhilarating news.

On Tuesday, July 12, 2012, Jill called Marcia to tell her about the call from Catholic Charities. There were a number of stunned people that week; after all, this information had been kept under lock and key for over five decades. Marcia knew that Jill had known about "the baby" for years, so the shocker for both of them was simply having Catholic Charities reaching out for its client. Other relatives in Clinton who heard about the phone call were just finding out about the fact that Marti even gave birth to another daughter. Finishing up her conversation with Jill, Marcia consented to discussing this further with Kim Laube.

The following day, Kim called Marcia to discuss how much she knew about having an older half-sister, or whether she knew anything at all. Marcia, understandably, was quite emotional about the contact but let Kim know that she was aware of this 1959 birth. Next, of course, was to see if she was interested in Kim passing her contact information on to me and connecting with me (as I write this, I feel like I'm discussing the possibility of making contact with aliens from another planet. Believe me when I say that *that* is exactly what it felt like).

When Marcia agreed that she would like to go forward, Kim explained that she would have to state her intentions in a letter and have it notarized. As timing would have it, Marcia had her hands full right then, primarily with her daughter Caitie getting her wisdom teeth pulled the next morning, Thursday. So . . . Marcia wrote the letter when she could squeeze it in, took care of Caitie and got her settled on Friday morning, then took off to the bank shortly after to get her document notarized. There happened to be a FedEx store next door, so she walked out of the bank and into the FedEx and had them scan her letter to Kim. Done!

❀ ❀ ❀

Each day of the following week seemed agonizingly long. I came home one afternoon in July, walked in our door, and sat down at the computer by the front window, the same one that I sat at the night that I emailed Catholic Charities for the first time. I guess there was something symbolic about checking at that spot to see if there was an email yet, because I would usually just check on my phone. I couldn't believe it. As soon as I logged on, my eyes went straight to an email from Kim. She had heard back from my sister, and not only did my sister *want* to talk, but she wanted to talk to me as soon as possible! When Kim asked her if she would like to connect with me sometime next week my sister said, "Next week!! How about in five minutes?"

In her emails to both of us, Kim had laid out all of our contact information, with the exception of home addresses. Now that I had the green light to move forward, I was shaking as I took a deep breath and looked at Marcia's cell. There it was right in front of me for the first time . . . my sister's name. My sister's cell number. Her email. Her hometown. Still shaking, I picked up my cell and dialed her number, a number that wasn't even saved in my phone but would soon be sitting in my "favorites." She immediately answered, and before even a few words could come out of my mouth, we both started crying. I was trying to just introduce myself and tell her my name—how odd, being fifty-two years old on this surreal phone call telling my own sister what my name was—when she broke in, maybe to help me compose myself.

"Kathe, I have known about you for twenty-four years."

Getting Acquainted

Years ago, in January 1989, Marcia was in the middle of one of the toughest times in her life. Her first marriage was not working out and she and her husband were separated. She was living with her parents (my birth mother and her husband, Bob) and she had two *very* young boys; the oldest was a year old and the second was a newborn. Marcia was just trying to make it through each day. Marti, sensing her daughter's unrelenting anguish, walked into the room where Marcia was that morning. As soon as Marcia looked at her mother, she knew it was serious. Marti just laid it out right then and there.

"Marcia, I know that you are going through a really tough time right now. I want to tell you about what happened to me when I was in my twenties. I gave up a baby for adoption in a different city and state from where I'd grown up. It was a girl. Back then, the nuns just told us to put it behind us—like we had no say in the matter. My boyfriend, who was the father, wanted to get married; I didn't."

Marcia remembered how very emotional her mom was, attempting to utter the details so very matter-of-factly, while the pain was evident in her face and even in the words that fell from her lips.

Marti finished her testament with, "Marcia, if I could get through that situation then, I *know* that you can make it through all of this."

❀ ❀ ❀

I remember thinking about how amazing it was that she had known about me for almost a quarter of a century . . . twenty-four years is a really long time. How could she not want to reach out? Had she been afraid of who she might find? That there'd be no "takebacks" after the truth had been discovered? Before I could dwell on these thoughts for more than a glimmer of a moment, I remembered a good friend telling me years ago that she, as the child who had been raised by her biological mother, found it exciting and amazing to find out that she had a sibling out there that she knew nothing about for decades. The difficulty in deciding whether to find that sister and make contact lay in one simple possibility: What if the adoptee had never been told that she was adopted? If that were the case, applying that to our situation, Marcia's reaching out to me could be enough to ruin my life . . . or, at the very least, take me for a major tumble, finding out that not only were my parents adoptive parents but that they had never even told me the truth. Fortunately, in my case, Chuck and Ruth Linn had always told me that I was adopted, since I was old enough to comprehend what that meant.

Marcia told me that first summer after we met that she never thought about telling anyone about my existence; she felt as if it wasn't her place to discuss it. Simply stated, it was her mother's story. Marcia felt that it was respectful to keep her mom's secret for her. She also said that she felt that if she had brought this up with other people, it would have made it more real, and therefore a greater loss for Marcia. She went on to explain that she didn't want me to think that she did not want to contact me, it was more a matter of being *afraid*. For a very long time, she didn't think about it—the whole situation—as having a sister out there somewhere. *Then* she went through a phase where she was mad because she felt that she'd never meet me. In Marcia's words:

"From early 1989 when my mom told me, until March of 2008, I put this information way in the back of my mind. When my aunt brought it up in 2008, it was the first time I thought of my mom's 'baby' as my sister. My cousin and my aunt were so kind when they brought it up, saying how wonderful it would be if the two of us could meet. So, for those four years (2008 until 2012), the thought of searching for MY sister became more and more of a possibility for me.

"I never brought up the topic with my mom again. She told me at the beginning of 1989, and she passed away December of 2002. When my mom told me, I really got the sense that she never wanted to talk about it again because it was so painful. I never considered asking her about it later. She didn't specifically ask me not to bring it up. She did say that my dad didn't know anything about it."

Once Marcia and I started talking daily on the phone during that summer and getting to know each other, I

could feel that it was important to her to be allowed to send a letter to my mom, who raised me. Between the many pictures I sent her of me growing up, as well as numerous stories, it didn't take long for Marcia to conclude that I'd had a wonderful upbringing and was loved very dearly by both of my parents. I sensed that there was some sort of healing on Marcia's part in knowing that her mother's loss had turned into an indescribable blessing for both my parents and for me, and, I'd like to think, for my brother as well. As Margaret had passed almost ten years ago, I think Marcia felt compelled to be the one to tell my mother Ruth Ann how thankful she was to find out that her mom's first baby had been taken care of so beautifully.

But here's the thing: my parents did not know about my birth mother search, let alone a newfound sister.

My dad had been diagnosed with dementia about three years prior, although we all knew that he had shown signs for years before that. His health remained fairly stable for years after his afflictions began, but that summer of 2012 was different. His decline became rapid, and I often found myself, every two to three weeks, driving back and forth the eight hours each way from Nashville to Fort Smith, Arkansas where they lived. It seemed unfathomable to me that we were on the short route to losing my dad just months after finding out who my birth mother was, along with the discovery that I had a sister. My dad was 6'3" and my mom was tiny: 5'3" with a small frame. He began to fall a lot and Mom could not pick him up.

Mom then hired two wonderful assistants, Naomi and Linda, to come in and help so Dad could stay home, but eventually it became too much for everyone to handle physically. Mom had to make the painful choice to place him in a nursing home for the last nine days of his life. As much as I wanted to tell my mom about what I had discovered about my birth mother and my sister, she was under an inordinate amount of stress that summer and fall, and that news would not be as exciting for her as it had been for me. It was important for me to tell her the truth and also to explain why and how it had happened, but that discussion would have to wait. With Dad's failing health, the time was simply not appropriate right then.

Marcia and I continued to get to know each other throughout the summer of 2012, through many calls, texts, and emails with all sorts of photos: old pictures of each of us growing up; photos she sent to me of my birth mother's childhood—we laughed at how much I looked like her; pictures of our families growing up; as well as pictures of our husbands and children. The first four photos of Margaret that she emailed to me were labeled, except for one. The first picture was one of Margaret as a baby. The second one was when she was three years old and sitting on the porch with a favorite stuffed animal. Under the third photo, Marcia just said she wasn't sure how old Margaret was there. The last was a beautiful picture of Margaret standing outside in her new nursing uniform and cap.

As this was the first time I had seen any images of my birth mother, it was pretty emotional for me, and astonishing to see our physical resemblance. As soon as I looked at the email, I called Marcia to tell her I knew with quite a bit of certainty how old Margaret was in that third shot.

"I think she was ten years old."

"How would you know that?" Marcia replied. I'm sure she found my certainty pretty odd.

"Marcia, as soon as I saw the third photo, I had to go search for a photo of me from my tenth birthday. When I showed Don, my husband, he just started laughing."

Marti and I looked almost identical in our two ten-year-old pictures, taken twenty-four years apart.

We even wore our hair in the same style—braided pigtails behind the ears. Our smiles revealed the same set of teeth. Extremely similar bone structure. Hazel-green eyes. A smattering of freckles across the nose and cheekbones. I told Marcia that I was texting her my pic next to Margaret's so she could see for herself. She had the same reaction that Don and I did; you had to laugh because we looked so much alike. And what were the odds of both headshots being taken at the same angle with the same braids?

What an absolute thrill this was for me . . . to look at a photo of someone else and see that we looked *so* very much alike. It may be hard for most people to see why this would be so exhilarating, but it had never happened to me *ever* during the first five decades of my entire life! Our daughters' looks were a mix of both of us, but Don's genes definitely dominated. That moment was a complete blessing for me, in such a very simple and heartwarming way.

It only took about a week or two into this "discovery" process for us to both realize how much we wanted to meet in person. The question was just *where* since we lived on opposite sides of the country from each other. During the week that Marcia and I were discussing this, one of my closest friends here in Nashville,

Margaret Martin, was listening to our incredible story and offered up her and her husband Phil's condo in Destin, Florida, for a week in August.

"Phil and I have a conflict that week and can't be there then. We would love to have our place be where you two met and got to know each other!"

I called Marcia to see what she thought about it. I could tell she was as excited about the idea as I was. The closest airport was Pensacola, so she started looking into flights. The timing of the week in August was perfect for both of our schedules. Not only that, but logistically it worked great for me too. Don and I were going to be dropping off our youngest daughter, Kat, for her freshman year at Tulane in New Orleans the day before the condo was available for our use. The drive from New Orleans to the Pensacola Airport was just a simple two-and-a-half hours. Things just kept falling into place, starting back on that day that the social worker had accidentally forgotten to white out my birth mother's maiden name in the packet from Catholic Charities.

Marcia booked her flight, and our "adventure" was right around the corner. There would be no one else on this trip except Marcia and me. Don flew home from New Orleans to give me this private time with my sister. He was extremely supportive of us going on this trip together, even as basic strangers. No husbands, no kids, just the two of us. I think he knew in his heart of hearts, just like I did, that everything was going to be okay. You must admit . . . deciding to spend five days anywhere with nearly a complete stranger is an unusual endeavor.

Before Marcia had booked her flights, I was full of anticipation and excitement that we were going to meet in person only a month and a half after we had first spoken to each other. Once the trip was booked, I found that my excitement about getting together hadn't waned, but the sense of eagerness was interspersed with thoughts of, "Am I completely nuts?? I don't really know this person at all . . . and we're spending *days* alone together?" Looking back on it, I believe that we both just put our trust in God and the universe that we were supposed to do this and that everything would be fine. I also know that I had a little divine nudge that first night that I sat in front of our computer, prompting me to look up the contact information for Des Moines Catholic Charities. It could have been one of my guardian angels, but it might have been my birth mother herself. I feel sure that she hoped her two daughters might meet one day.

Meet You at the Baggage Claim

A t the end of that week in August 2012, Hurricane Isaac was barreling over Haiti and Cuba, getting ready to roll over the Florida Keys before heading into the Gulf of Mexico. The storm was predicted to hit somewhere between the Florida panhandle and New Orleans. If Isaac made landfall in New Orleans as was now forecasted, Kat and her whole freshman class would experience their first week of college in a storm lockdown. If the hurricane turned toward the Florida panhandle and Destin, Marcia's and my first time together would turn into an evacuation instead of hanging out at the beach. But we decided that we would have the chance to get to know each other regardless of what the five days together had in store for us weather-wise.

After Don and I got Kat organized to start her college career at Tulane, I churned like a hurricane of mixed emotions. We had just officially "empty nested" with the beginning of our baby's first semester of college. As I drove out of New Orleans and toward Pensacola, I wanted to cry over Kat growing up so incredibly fast, but was also elated with the anticipation of meeting my sister who I'd only recently found. There I was, driving down the highway by myself, distraught over Kat already being in college, then minutes later being so thankful that she was absolutely thrilled to be there. Combine those thoughts with a sister I was about to meet just down the road . . . the emotions that I felt during that relatively short drive bounced around in my head, back and forth, like a ball in a pinball machine.

It was hard to believe that I would actually be in the presence of my "new" sibling in a little over two hours. Normally the drive from New Orleans is very easy and flies by since it's under three hours. That day, I remember it just seemed to go on relentlessly due to my eagerness to meet Marcia, my sister of forty-eight years.

I pulled into the parking lot at the Pensacola Airport and suddenly simple actions became difficult. Although we had driven through Pensacola several times, I had never been to the airport. The ordinary task of figuring out where I was supposed to park was absurdly comical. I couldn't focus on the signs pointing me to the correct area for simply picking up an arriving passenger. We are *not* talking about a large parking lot here. I had to circle around a few times to get it right, but finally managed to park.

I sat in the parking lot, waiting for Marcia's text that she had landed. Unbeknownst to me, my sister had had the foresight to charge and bring a camcorder on her flight. As the plane was making its final descent, she turned to the complete stranger next to her and asked the gentleman if he would mind videotaping her meeting her sister for the first time. He paused, probably quite puzzled by how that could be—meeting for the first time well into adulthood—and then he declined. He probably just thought Marcia was crazy, given how bizarre the request was.

After Marcia deplaned and was walking toward the baggage claim, she looked around for a hopefully kind stranger and asked a woman walking next to her if she would please record this event. Imagine the surprise on this woman's face . . . she's being asked by a stranger who has to be at least in her forties to document the *introduction* of two middle-aged sisters! The lady graciously agreed to do so without even asking a question, besides, "Are you sure you trust me with this?" Marcia said that the newly-appointed videographer could tell that this was an extremely important event, and it was probably best to leave it at that.

At the Pensacola airport, the baggage claim is at the entrance of the building near the parking lot. Marcia had texted me as soon as she landed, so I walked inside a few minutes later, knowing that she would be walking toward baggage pickup. A few more minutes later I saw her coming down the escalator, and although we were at opposite ends of the room, our eyes immediately went to each other. By this point, we had seen enough pictures of each other that there was no doubt who each of us was looking for. The fact that we were probably two of the tallest women in the baggage area made it easy to spot each other. The physical similarities were swiftly apparent: she is 5'10" and I am 6'0." We both have blond to strawberry-blond straight hair, although she wears hers longer than mine. The same freckly fair skin. Eyes both green to hazel.

I guess I wasn't ready for how emotional this moment would be. As soon as we saw each other Marcia began to cry, and I was on the verge of doing the same. As we hurried toward each other, I felt the tears falling fast. I vaguely remember seeing the kind lady keeping her distance but slowly walking behind my sister, filming the whole thing. By the time we reached each other and embraced in a very long, almost-clutching hug, Marcia was sobbing, which set me off as well. Looking back on this scene, we must have been quite the spectacle for all of the passengers simply trying to retrieve their luggage and get on with their trips. At that moment, though, there was no one around us staring, no one filming. All sounds and motion around us stopped. It was just a very poignant and emotional meeting between two sisters, half a century overdue.

CHAPTER 6

"New" Sisters

The drive from the airport to Destin is an hour and a half. To me it seemed to fly by; we had so much to talk about. It was the exact opposite of my drive to pick up Marcia, which seemed to go on forever. By this point we knew quite a bit about each other, because we had spent hours, days, and weeks on the phone asking questions about our lives growing up, the places we had lived, our immediate and extended families, and any topic one could imagine while trying to play catch-up with a sibling after almost five decades.

By the time we arrived in Destin, the weather reports were beginning to look ominous. The winds

97

had picked up and would continue to escalate considerably in the coming days. Although Isaac made landfall in two parts of Louisiana, its effects were evident for days all along the Gulf of Mexico. The condo, which was on the beach, seemed to be the best and possibly only place to be, as we looked out the windows at the mighty roar of the Gulf's waves and winds. We'd had the foresight to stop and pick up some groceries, not knowing how much we would be able to drive around in the coming days. I remember us driving down the street, just half a mile, to one of our family's favorite Mexican restaurants, where we had eaten several times when vacationing in the area. Our plan was to pick up dinner and bring it back to the condo. No one was on the street, and I was shocked that the restaurant was even open. The usual bright and lively atmosphere of the foyer was quiet and subdued, with barely a skeleton crew of employees there. I thought to myself, as I picked up our bag of food, "These employees must live very close to the restaurant!"

I laughed to myself the first night after we said goodnight and were getting ready to go to bed. We each had our own bedrooms, and although we had spent so much time over the summer getting to know each other through conversations, texts, and emails, I had this fleeting thought that I had just committed to spending four days and five nights with a stranger. Of course, this wasn't entirely true—she was my sister, albeit my *new* one, and as Karin, one of my best friends, so succinctly put it when I told her about our story, "Kathe, this is not just anyone. You two were formed in the same womb!" So . . . I put my mind at rest. My sister was one of the kindest, most loving people I had ever met. I'm sure she had the same concerns about hanging out with me, but we both made the commitment to make this work.

Our time together at the beach involved very little stepping on the sand or even getting near the water. The winds and waves became quite violent, and because of Kat and all of our relatives in New Orleans, we had the Weather Channel on the TV most of every day just to know what was going on. Even though we were not able to relax on the beach, it became a precious time for us to get to know each other in person. I found myself just utterly amazed in the middle of conversations . . . here we were, sitting together for days, talking about such ordinary things, yet it all felt extraordinary. This so very easily could have never happened—my sister and I meeting anywhere at any time, let alone right here.

It was fascinating to learn of little habits or idiosyncrasies that we had in common. At one point we were sitting in the den talking and we both had throw pillows on our laps. This is something I've done for as long as I can remember when sitting around—and there's Marcia sitting across from me doing the same thing.

Lying in bed, putting the leg closest to the edge over the blanket while the rest of your body is under the blanket. Genetic, possibly? Who knows for sure, but once we noticed these tiny little things it delighted us that we had these odd habits in common.

One afternoon it was a bit calmer outside, so we ventured out to the boardwalk where there are rows of built-in wooden benches, providing a tranquil place to sit quietly, watching the waves. All seemed so peaceful, but then I realized that Marcia was crying softly. I asked her what was wrong—it kind of shocked me. She was looking down at my feet. She cried, "You said on the phone that your eyes are green, Kathe. But really, they are hazel with yellow flecks exactly like our mother's. Your feet are exactly the same as hers. Your toes, the shape of your feet . . . everything!"

At that moment the only other humans within eyesight walked up on the boardwalk, a mother with her young son. They apparently had just come out to see the crashing waves and were not intending to go any closer. Upon seeing Marcia's weeping and me holding her hand, the mom hastily ushered her little one down the steps and away from us, as if we had cooties. I thanked God for this perfectly-timed moment of comic relief that made both of us suddenly break out in laughter!

Another one of our limited outings away from the condo was to go get our first pedicure together. We wandered over to a nail salon that I had been to a few times with my daughters during family summer beach trips. After we walked in, we both looked through the nail colors, and after I had picked a new color that I'd never seen before, I showed it to Marcia and said that I was going with this new, bright color because it just *looked* like summer and the beach, plus the name of it was "Flip Flop Fantasy." Marcia had a few colors in her hand that she was debating on using. When she looked down at my new beachy color, she decided to go with the same. So, the brand-new sisters had our toes painted the same color. Because the color reminds me so much of her, I have had my toenails painted this same color every summer since then, a tradition I plan to carry on indefinitely.

The rest of the trip was mostly indoors, catching up on decades of our lives and getting to know each other better. We of course were looking forward to future trips—me flying to Phoenix to see her home and meet her family, Marcia flying to Nashville to do the same, and even a trip to Clinton, Illinois where my birth mother grew up. It would be fascinating to see where Margaret was born and raised, where she went to school, her family homes, and even where she had her horses. Many of her relatives still lived in Clinton, including Jill, my "new" cousin who happened to answer the phone that very special day in 2012.

Marcia's flight out on our last day together was very early in the morning. The plan was for us to pack up and leave together; I would drive her to the Pensacola airport and then just keep on driving back home to Nashville. It was so dark the whole drive to the airport that I felt like it was the middle of the night. I was dreading saying goodbye to her. Even though we had spent less than five days together, and we had committed to the aforementioned trips in the future, we had no idea when we would actually see each other again.

I pulled up to the curb at the airport and we took Marcia's bags out of the back of my car. I was amazed at how much my heart was aching about saying goodbye. It was so wonderful that we miraculously ended up finding each other, but we also lived two thirds of the country away from each other. We embraced in a long, tight hug before she quickly turned and grabbed her luggage at the same time that I jumped back into my car. In my estimation, a quick exit is the best way to go after an emotional goodbye. From inside my car, I watched as she pulled her suitcase until she strolled through the sliding glass door, enveloped by the terminal. She was there by my side for four days and now she wasn't. Off she went, back to Phoenix, my blessed accidental sister.

Not long after our first meeting and trip to the beach, Marcia began working on a beautiful scrapbook

At dinner—Kathe on right, Marcia on left

commemorating this significant time together. She completely surprised me with it when she mailed the album to me in early November 2012, along with a DVD of events showing my birth mother alive and in motion—talking, walking, dancing! The following excerpts are from this scrapbook, as Marcia wrote them, verbatim.

On Our Initial Meeting

Kathe and I met at the Pensacola airport on Sunday, August 26, 2012. I was so excited to see her that I didn't want to bother with the video camera I had brought along to document our first time to see each other. I asked a woman on my flight if she would videotape me meeting my sister for the first time. She did a great job, then Kathe and I were so caught up in each other that we never really explained to her why we were just meeting at this age!

It was so great to finally meet Kathe! I had waited 24 years and I could not believe my eyes. I actually backed up when I saw her. She was so beautiful, so precious to me.

It was about an hour-long drive to Destin, and it was a beautiful, sunny day. We checked into the condo and then went to a restaurant called The Back Porch for dinner. We took pictures on the beach right in front of the restaurant, and we later discussed that it felt like "The Twilight Zone." It was somewhat strange for Kathe to realize that she had a sister, and for me to meet someone who I never thought I would get to meet, not to mention who looks so much like our mom!

On The Value of Spending Time Together

The next day, we took a walk on the beach and had a bite to eat. After lunch we went to Winn Dixie, a grocery store. It was so sweet to me to do something so simple as to go grocery shopping with my sister. I felt so comfortable with her.

The Inevitable Emotional Side Coming Out

When we got back to the condo, we took showers and then sat out on the condo patio. I couldn't hold it in any longer, how much she looks like our mom! Something about her damp hair and her eyes, oh my goodness! I just started to cry because it felt so strange to see someone so very similar in looks to my mom, whom I loved so much, sitting right in front of me! Her eyes are identical; her arms, hands, legs, feet, freckles, and her smile are too. It is really amazing. It was emotional because we both felt so sad for our mom and the pain she suffered by giving Kathe up for adoption.

That evening we got take-out from a delicious Mexican restaurant which was just down the road. We watched videos of our mom next. The tear-jerker for both of us was the one of our mom dancing in 1966. Wow! What a beautiful mommy. She was so very happy in the video, and she loved me so much; you could tell by the way she looked at me when I came into the video. It was really indescribable to be showing Kathe a video of her birth mom, at an age close to the time when Kathe was born. I am so glad that the two of them will meet in heaven one day because it is hard to think of all they missed in their lives without each other.

The whole evening was pretty emotional. We also watched another video of Mom dancing, this one from Christmas 2001. I gave Kathe a lock of Mom's hair, a pillow cover embroidered with "Margaret Maurer," and some pictures of our mom when she was a girl. Kathe looked just like her when they were both about ten years old.

The Advent of Our Dual Sleuthing, Right There at the Beach

Later that night we started looking up information about Kathe's birth father online. We looked through some Missouri college yearbooks because we knew that he had played football in college but at that point we weren't sure where. We didn't go to bed until 2:00 a.m. It was so sweet to be just across the hall from my precious sister and to be able to say "goodnight" in person.

The next day we were in no hurry to get going. We searched for Maureen Hagan for any contact information, especially her phone number, online. She was an old nursing friend of our mom's who probably knew, or at least knew about, Kathe's birth father.

We continued to look for any kind of contact for Maureen in the following days. We just couldn't help ourselves regarding the sleuthing. Eventually, I did find a number and we both decided that I would call. I was able to talk to her very kind husband who said that Maureen was indeed still alive but had very advanced dementia and didn't even know who he was. That was disheartening to be so close but then run into a dead end.

Sharing Old Videos and Albums

While in the condo, we looked at her photo albums of Kathe's family from when her girls were little. She also brought photo albums from when she grew up, so I also got to see baby pictures of Kathe with her adoptive parents! How special that was to me. We got ready and went down to The Back Porch again. We took some pictures there and we told the waitress we were sisters who had just met!

We returned to the condo that evening where we watched more videos. We watched the video of Mike's and my wedding, our youngest daughter Megan's actual day of birth at the hospital, and one of my two boys, Chris and Michael, when they were little. We decided to watch the one of Mom dancing in 1966 once again. We had so much fun, laughing and eating home-baked cookies and drinking wine. We laughed when we noticed that our mom didn't bother to put down her cigarette while she was dancing!

A Poignant Spiritual Moment

We fed the seagulls and then sat on the dock and watched the tumultuous waves breaking along the shore. All of a sudden, I felt like my mom had been sitting beside me about two seconds prior. I could hear her voice, like when we were at the beach at Rocky Point, Mexico. Then I looked over and saw Kathe's feet, which look exactly like our mom's! I couldn't help but cry again.

What an unforgettable experience! How precious to be able to not only meet each other after all these years, but to be able to spend five nights and four days on a beautiful beach together, uninterrupted, and unhurried. I will always be so thankful for this trip and for being able to meet my wonderful sister!

Meeting
Margaret Maurer

D uring the summer of 2012, Marcia and I were on another one of our *long* phone conversations, continuing to get to know each other. Marcia mentioned to me that she had been looking through Margaret's memorabilia and remembered that she had original journals written by our mother, with writings that began with details of the day that my birth mother was born! She went on to describe her life events, family, and relationships from beginning to almost the end. Her last journal entry was in November 2000, and she left this earthly world in December 2002, so the content encompassed the vast majority of her life. Marcia decided to take the diaries to a printer to make copies for me. I couldn't believe how lucky I was to have had a birth mother, whom I'd never met, who decided to chronicle her life. I may not have had the chance to meet her and thank her in person, but what an incredible gift to receive one hundred seventy-two pages of personal chronicles from her!

This also allows you insight into how thoughtful my sister is. Marcia had the first journal copied and bound in August 2012. It wasn't until I looked back on the letter she had written to send with the journal that I saw Marcia had written and sent it on my dad, Chuck Linn's, last living birthday.

The following is her verbatim letter sent with the first of the three copied spirals, dated August 9, 2012.

Kathe,

I am so excited for you to receive this first journal! As you know, Mom wrote two journals, but I will be making them into three because her first journal had so many more pages filled in than her second journal.

Anyway, you will receive a total of three—the second two have about sixty pages in each. (I just haven't made them yet, but I will within the next few days.)

I am so thankful she wrote these—I know they will bless you, and as we talked about, you can really learn about the wonderful person she was through her own words.

Love,

Marcia

When my sister called me to tell me that she was sending the first of these journals, she told me a story from years previous regarding these writings. Marcia said that she first heard about the journals from Margaret when she was in the middle of writing them. Then, when my birth mother became sick, she handed them over to Marcia. During the years following Margaret's death in 2002, Marcia shared the journals with those closest to her, telling them about what they entailed. On two separate occasions, Marcia's husband, Mike, and one of her best friends growing up, opined that since Marcia knew everything that was in the journals, it made sense that she probably wrote them for the baby she had given up for adoption. Whether that was my birth mother's intent or not, this now grown-up baby could not be more grateful!

I've been in possession of my copies for over nine years. I consider them to be amongst my most important material possessions, and can tell you that if there was a fire in our house and I had five minutes to pick up what I wanted to keep, I would grab our daughters' baby pictures and our wedding photos, then add my birth mother's journals to those armfuls. That is why I always know where they are in our home. I sat down recently to read them again, from beginning to end. I don't recall previously noticing how many similarities there were in her upbringing and mine. The physical similarities—tall, blond to strawberry blond, hazel eyes with a smattering of freckles, and the same build—could certainly be expected to be passed on from a mother to her child. It was so many other aspects that suddenly surprised me.

Our birth weight was nearly identical, which is interesting in two completely different generations of pregnancy care and obstetrics. We both started kindergarten at four years old and entered high school at thirteen years old. She mentions in several excerpts about her tendency to be a "crier." Check. We both had an inclination toward the sciences and medicine, but she specifically pointed out that her *least* favorite science class ever was chemistry. My truth exactly. She was an artist her entire life. Most of my life I just assumed that my interest in art and creative projects came from my adoptive mom, Ruth Ann. Obviously this was a case where nature and nurture converged!

Margaret described her dad as tall, blond, and handsome with a dry sense of humor. Sounds like my adoptive dad, Chuck. Margaret wrote, "Daddy was generous, money-wise with his children, but more importantly, very interested and concerned with our lives. He was a low-key sort of parent but also very subtly persuasive when there was an issue. *And* he talked to us. How important that was!" It's interesting seeing this perspective from her, while knowing she didn't feel comfortable ever sharing her first pregnancy with her parents.

By this point in reading her memoirs, I felt as if she was projecting into the future and describing my adoptive dad. Once again, there were so many similarities. She even mentioned that as a car dealer, having his pick of many different cars, her dad definitely had a car of choice, a four-door Cadillac. Funny that my dad drove the same the whole time I lived at home (primarily because his best friend owned a dealership, just like Margaret's dad, so that's where the best deal was!). Her mother was diminutive and had brunette hair, just like my adoptive mom. Margaret said, "Mom was most of all, a character." Check.

She even told a story in the journals about how by the time she entered high school she was six inches taller than her mother, and how she thought her mom must have felt pretty silly disciplining her when Margaret "was towering over her." I remember vividly standing in our kitchen when I was thirteen or fourteen years old, with my mom chastising me for something I shouldn't have done. I stood even closer to her and looked *way* down at her. Fortunately, she found the humor in it instead of grounding me for insubordination. It was absurd how I loomed over her by the time I was twelve. By the time I was fully grown, I was six feet tall. My mom always said she was 5'3", but I think she was stretching the truth by a full inch or two.

Both of my parents grew up in a small, midwestern town, as did Margaret's mom and dad. All four of the Maurer children were baptized Catholic, as were my brother and I. She described her mother as deeply spiritual and devout in her Catholic faith her entire life, a faith that got her through some brutally tough times and unexpected personal losses. My mother's spirituality ran deep all her life and kept her alive when she was expected to die from a ruptured appendix at twenty years old. She later spent fourteen months in intensive care at the age of forty, due to complications from the appendix issues two decades earlier. She came home from the Mayo Clinic, against all odds, weighing seventy-eight pounds. Through years of recovery, Mom asked for healing and believed she would receive it, and miraculously, she did. She too never wavered from her Catholic faith.

These parts in the journals about the faith that ran deep in Marti's family and her comments about her dad's generosity and his involvement in all his children's lives caused me to try to decipher the puzzle of her decision. Why, in a family so close, would Marti be resolved not to tell her parents about her pregnancy? Was this about expectations they had for her, or did it have more to do with their Catholic faith . . . or both? Or neither? I know that Margaret loved her parents; that is clearly apparent throughout the course of her journals. Not to mention all that Marcia had told me about the tight family connections. Yet, I was still struck by how she couldn't share her pregnancy with them. I decided to turn to Marcia to see if she had any more insight, or if she simply had her own contemplations about our shared mom. I am so thankful that I asked.

"I believe that her parents would have been very supportive of her," Marcia explained. "I kind of think that she panicked and acted in haste by not telling them originally. And then I think that as time went on, it just seemed easier to have fewer people know. I would bet, though, that looking back she would have told them if she had it to do all over again."

This came from a woman who knew her grandparents and mother very well, so I trust her thoughts on how they might have dealt with this. It gave me a perspective that probably was already hiding in the deep recesses of my mind, wondering how this convoluted story would have played out had there been some more, albeit painful, communication. How different our lives would have been had Marti had a "do-over." The thought of having had the opportunity to grow up with Marcia fills me with unbounded joy, but the bittersweet thought of a life without my parents, my brother, or my grandparents . . . The life I knew previous to this point would have been a completely different existence. Logically, it's impossible to miss the people in my life that were never there. Being in possession of this information about the circumstances of my birth makes me even more grateful for the family I had growing up... but I also know how fortunate I am to have time with Marcia.

Take that one step further: had my birth parents decided to marry as was discussed, I would have grown up in my biological family and then Marcia wouldn't have been Marcia! It's hard to even imagine, but I do believe that Marti's tipping point was not an *accident;* things worked out as planned.

I had a good laugh with my sister about two ways that Margaret and I could not be more different. Her mother, my birth grandmother, had a love of horses that she passed on to Margaret. She talks at some length in her journals about her great passion for her horses, especially Likely Lady, a breathtaking sorrel whom her parents finally decided to break down and buy for her. Margaret referred to encountering Lady as a moment of love at first sight for her. She rode and cared for her throughout high school, and kept her in a pasture not far from their house that belonged to a relative.

I, on the other hand, had a close call with a horse's hoof to my back at a very young age on one of my dad's coworker's farms. I have always found horses to be exquisite to behold, but to behold at a distance! Ask my equestrian friends and they will chuckle at my inability to relax around even the most docile of fillies or mares. It was nothing short of a miracle when I finally fed my dear niece Tori's horse a carrot for the first time about ten years ago. You would have thought that Tori was training me for a marathon it took so long . . . and she couldn't stop laughing when I accomplished the mission!

The other huge dissimilarity between my birth mother and me is her fascination with flying. Like in a plane. I have no problem with my dreams where I'm flying way above Earth as a bird, coasting along on a clear, sunny day. That's because there's no turbulence. I would never miss a trip because I had to fly, I'd just pray for a smooth-as-glass flight with no bumps. Then if my poor hubby Don was on the flight with me, nine times out of ten he would deplane with a gouge in his left arm where I'd cut off his circulation hanging on for dear life.

On the other hand, in her journals Margaret tells of how she flew on a plane for the first time to come home for Christmas, from Denver to Chicago. She had just turned twenty-five and the plane was very delayed due to it hitting a portable flight of stairs while taxiing. By the time the plane finally got to Chicago, her parents were both nervous wrecks waiting at O'Hare Airport, while Margaret couldn't wait to tell them how she was fascinated with flying. She remained enamored with it for the rest of her life.

There is one other entry in Margaret's journals that blew me away. This was about the details of Marcia's birth.

"The due date was on the weekend, so my doctor convinced me to be induced. It was a painful labor with intense back pain. I finally submitted to some pain medication about an hour before Marcia was born. Labor lasted about four hours. Anyway, our baby girl was born weighing only five pounds, eight ounces. At first, she didn't cry and I heard the doctor say that there was a very long cord and it had been wrapped around her neck three times. This can be fatal. In a couple of minutes, she started crying and was okay. I knew from my experience as an OB nurse that this cord situation was very dangerous. I thanked God right then and there for being induced when I was and having a good outcome."

I have read and reread this entry of Margaret's journals several times. So many fortunate events helped my sister and I finally meet decades into our lives. Right there, at the moment of Marcia's birth, her life could have easily ended. How blessed I am that she made it.

CHAPTER 8

Questions
Unanswered

The lucky breakthrough of not having my birth mother's maiden name whited out was a catalyst. One that set me on fire to find my birth mother, eventually leading me to Marcia. However, all I really knew about my birth father was limited to what little was sent to me from Catholic Charities in my file, and the tidbits that my mom, Ruth, had told me at lunch when I was twenty-two.

I was home for a visit when Mom and I decided to go get one of our favorite sandwiches for lunch at an old

Des Moines staple, The Tavern. *I* thought we were there to get our "Italian grinder" fix, but halfway through our meal, Mom dropped a bomb on me.

My parents had never really talked about my birth parents or Jamie's birth parents growing up. The one odd thing my mother did bring up occasionally over our teen years was the fact that Jamie's birth mom was just sixteen years old when she gave birth to him. I recall my mom telling me when I was young that she and Dad had very little information about my birth parents, which was very typical of closed adoptions. That lack of discussion must have suited both my brother and me just fine, as we didn't feel compelled to bring it up ourselves either.

Being adopted came up from time to time, primarily in discussions with new people that we met or doctors who asked about the medical history of our parents and grandparents. But at this moment, when my mom suddenly asked if I'd like to know what little she and Dad knew about my birth parents, the shock on my face must have been obvious. Of course, she had now piqued my interest and I couldn't wait to hear what she had to say.

The conversation about them was short but intriguing, and all I remembered about that discussion for years to come was: Birth mother, thirty-seven, nurse. Birth father, twenty-six, water skier. These were just small morsels of information that Mom (somewhat inaccurately) recalled had come up during my parents' conversations with the folks at Catholic Charities during the adoption process. Mom had waited until just after I had graduated from college to disseminate this information to me. I guess her line of thinking might have been, "She's an adult now. I think she can handle this."

Mom mentioned that my birth father had been a champion water skier around the time I was born. Today, that fact combined with a first and last name would have probably facilitated a pretty easy search, but not the case when such records were not online. So . . . between the adoption file I had just received and my mom's comments from three decades before, I now had a vague physical description, plus a few other tidbits: Robert S. Six foot three. Dark wavy hair, green eyes, twenty-three when I was born. Clearly too little information to search further on my end, not to mention that my original intention in electing to search at all was to discover some of the medical history that my three daughters, Lauren, Carolyn, and Kat, were missing.

Interesting how the mind works as the secrets unfold; once I accidentally found out my birth mother's maiden last name, I was possessed to find out her married name, if indeed she had married and changed her surname. Once I had her details, I found myself wanting to know the full name of her boyfriend, my birth father.

A clue to solving that mystery emerged shortly after I met Marcia.

During one of our first talks during the summer of 2012, Marcia and I were discussing the possibility of finding out my birth father's name. She was just as interested—maybe even more interested than me, because after all, this was her mother's past, and a part of Margaret's life that she knew nearly nothing about. She remembered something that Aunt Rita, Margaret's younger and closest sister in age, had shared with Marcia years ago.

In March 2008, Jill had invited Marcia and her family to a surprise seventieth birthday party for Rita. Rita's health was declining, so Marcia made the effort to get there for the surprise. A few days into her visit, Rita told Marcia she had something serious she needed to talk to her about, concerning her mother. The look on her aunt's face was very grave. Marcia's response, at such a weighty moment, still cracks me up.

"Aunt Rita—how bad could what you have to tell me possibly be? She's already dead . . . it can't get much worse than that, *right?*"

Rita went on to tell Marcia that her mom had become pregnant by her boyfriend of six months, had given birth to a baby girl in 1959, and had given her up for adoption. Since they'd been dating for several months, the whole family knew him, so it wasn't a surprise that Rita could give Marcia a few facts about him. Of course, Marcia had already heard this from our mother, but listened politely because she could tell it was difficult for Rita to tell her about this. She took notes, which she was able to share with me.

Rita told her that Margaret had moved to Des Moines, Iowa with a nursing friend whose mother or grandmother lived there. She had graduated from nursing school in 1956. The baby (that would be me) was younger than Stan (Rita and Duane's oldest child) but older than Doug (their middle child). Rita was almost positive that the baby had been born in the fall of 1959.

Then came the notes about my birth father: Rita was sure of his name—Robert Stewart—

but not the spelling. She remembered him being a car salesman from Rantool, Illinois. She noted

that he had grown up in a small town in Missouri about an hour and a half or two hours outside

of Kansas City, a town that began with a "C." Rita recalled that someone had said that my birth father had played football in college, part of his undergrad at a university in Iowa and the other portion at a college in Missouri.

At this point, I felt I had enough information to really get digging. Just as I had when I started searching online for my birth mother's married name and location, I dropped everything in my life to track down his name, location, and any possible photos of this man, my birth father. My motive for this search was very different from that of seeking out my birth mother. With Margaret, I felt compelled to simply meet her and tell her thank you from the depths of my soul for giving me the best chance at a loving upbringing. In the case of my birth father, it was more a curiosity of wanting to see pictures, to see if we resembled each other, and of course the opportunity to get medical history for our daughters from that side of my biological family.

I was and have always remained a daddy's daughter, and loved my adoptive dad beyond words. My two searches were alike in that I wasn't looking for a "parent replacement" in either case, but they were different because I felt an overwhelming sense of gratitude toward one but just a simple curiosity about the other. For five decades, I'd had few emotions where either of my birth parents were concerned. Maybe those emotions were just suppressed, or maybe I'd never had the catalyst to make me think about or look for my birth parents. Either way, my feelings about them had come a long way in a very short time.

So . . . in the fall of 2012 I started putting together my search for this elusive man. Because of the information in my Catholic Charities file, I now knew how old Robert was when I was born, which made it pretty easy to figure out the approximate four years that he attended college. Since the file stated that he was born in 1936 and had graduated from Missouri State, I started looking through online yearbooks for Missouri State from 1953 through 1958 to see what I could find, especially on the football teams. When I didn't find his name there, I fanned out my search to other colleges and universities in Missouri and Iowa. I looked online relentlessly for days, sorting through online yearbooks from universities in those two states. I saw more photos of college football players from the 1950s than I ever wanted to think about.

I found several young men on football teams with similar names but no Robert Stewart. I also found a few young men in team photos of different sports with variations of his name, a Rob, a Bob, and people with similar last names or one of the possible spellings for his last name. The limitation of this "method" of research was that not all universities and colleges in Iowa and Missouri had gone back and added information online as far back as the 1950s. This tried my patience, but also fueled me on to other means of sleuthing.

It was logical to me to look through obituaries for people with his last name in Missouri. It was the same route I used at the beginning of my search for Marti. Either I would find out that he was already deceased, or an obituary of an immediate relative would mention him as a survivor. I got lucky with this one: not only did I find an obituary for an immediate family member, but the survivors were listed with their city and state of residence! Still no pic, but it was easy to get an actual street address once I knew the city and state. This would come in handy if I decided to formally request a birth father search.

The waterskiing comment from my mom, Ruth, had always seemed intriguing, so I went down that avenue to see what I could find. I found the Missouri Waterski Federation online and spent some time searching through state records. As I looked through records from current years (the first thing that popped up when I went to the website) I became much more intrigued. There were a number of records held by both females and males with the last name of Stewart. I wasn't expecting to find this last name in current records, but it certainly piqued my interest. However, archived records were not included on the website, so I couldn't access decades-old records online. Although this search did not take much time, it became apparent to me that I was becoming more invested by the day in discovering not just the identity of my birth mother but my birth father as well. A far cry from me thinking that I only wanted medical history for my children!

I then decided to look online at whatever high schools existed back in 1950s small-town Missouri. I figured that, with the small size of these towns beginning with a "C," there couldn't be but one or two high schools in each town and I would be limited to what yearbooks were published online.

During this picture search, I found a new sleuthing partner. Marcia was actually the first one to find a current photo of my birth father, in an article from the high school that he and his wife's children had all attended in California. There was a photograph of him surrounded by his whole family, honoring his and his wife's many years of support of that school. Although I didn't find the right high school yearbook right away, I eventually figured out the correct high school and the year that Robert was a senior there and ordered my own copy of my birth father's senior yearbook, simply to see one picture of him relatively close to when I was born. Between my sister's and my own on-and-off research, we managed to find one picture of him at eighteen years old and another one of him at seventy-six years old. Although the photos were found years apart and the age difference between the images was massive, it was clear to me that we had found the same man. Although I look primarily like my birth mother, I had no doubt at that point where I had inherited my high cheekbones, my long, straight nose, and my height from.

Finding a few photos and learning a little bit about Robert seemed to quench our thirst for information during our 2012 search. However, a few years after Marcia found the first photo of Robert, her second son and his fiancée were making plans for a destination wedding. When my sister and I were talking about the timing of their wedding one day, she told me that they had decided to get married on the beach in San Diego, California. I started laughing and said to her, "What are the odds?"

By this point, it had been a while since I'd learned Robert's current address. It was in California, in a suburb of San Diego. How ironic that of all of the beautiful destinations Michael and Meagan could have chosen, they picked one a few miles from my birth father's house! Marcia, her husband Mike, and their youngest, my niece Megan, drove by his house the day after the wedding, as it was so close by. It was pretty surreal to me to be on the phone with her as she drove by. Why? I guess because, just like finding out more and more details about Marti, the more I found out about Robert, the more he became a real person—not just this nondescript person who'd been tucked in the back crevices of my mind for so long.

Remember Kim Laube, the incredible social worker that helped me through this whole discovery process? In November 2012, I had put together enough information about who my birth father was and how to contact him that I called Kim and formally requested a birth father search. This was probably a bit of an unusual request, because everything I had discovered about this man in California was adding up to the strong probability that I had found the right guy. That meant rather than asking Kim to begin researching and attempting to hunt down my birth father as she had to do with my birth mother, I was handing her the necessary information to identify and contact him. I could have picked up the phone and called him myself for free, but it was worth every penny of the fee to ask Kim to do it instead. Receiving a phone call like that from an agency would be enough to give anyone a heart attack, so I felt that hearing directly from me was that much more intense. Plus, by this point I had immense faith in Kim to be my intermediary for anything.

On Thanksgiving morning, within two weeks of my making my request to Kim, my dear dad, Chuck Linn, passed from this earthly plane. Literally two days later,

Kim called me to tell me that she had gotten in contact with Robert Stewart and a very interesting conversation ensued. According to Kim, when a man answered the phone, she introduced herself and asked if the man was Robert Stewart. He confirmed that he was, and they spoke from there. She relayed the rest of their conversation to me.

※ ※ ※

"This is a very confidential conversation, sir," Kim stated. "If you are not alone, I'd like to set up a day and time when you can talk in private. Is now good or should this wait?"

A bit of a pause on the other end, then Robert said, "I am alone."

"Is this the Robert Stewart who was born and raised in [C-town], Missouri?"

"Yes, it is."

"And did you attend [C-town] High School and graduate from Missouri State?"

"Yes."

In my humble opinion, it is intriguing to note that after these very direct questions outlining known facts about his life, he didn't stop to ask Kim what she was getting at. As Kim was relaying this to me, *two* days after my sweet dad had passed, I couldn't help but think what it would be like to be in Robert's mind while answering *yes* to each of these questions.

"Mr. Stewart, did you date Margaret Maurer, originally from Clinton, Illinois, for several months in late 1958 and early 1959?"

"Yes, I did. I remember Margaret. How is she?"

"I'm sorry to say that she is deceased. I'm actually calling on someone else's behalf."

I could only imagine the size of the gulp that must have engulfed his throat at that moment. I was honestly surprised that he didn't end the conversation or hang up on Kim, but possibly he was very curious about what was coming next. To this point in the conversation, he had been a man of very few words.

"Mr. Stewart, my client has hired me to conduct a search for her birth father. She has specific information about herself and her life that she would like to share with him. We believe that you are her father."

"Ms. Laube, I never had sexual relations with Margaret Maurer, so I couldn't be the birth father."

"If you are sure about that, Mr. Stewart, then this conversation is over. I want you to hold on to my number in case you change your mind about what you've said or have anything else regarding this case that you would like to discuss." At this point,

Kim was thinking that the conversation was coming to an end.

"Ms. Laube, is she happy? Is she married? Does she have children?"

"Sir, the information that she has shared with me is that which she wants her birth father to know. Since you have stated that you are not her birth father, I cannot reveal any of her personal information to you. If you change your mind and want to talk about this at a later date, you know where to find me."

This was now the second time during my family searches that Kim Laube had run into something that had never happened before in all her years in the business of adoption and searches. The first was calling Margaret's sister's house, having Jill answer the phone, stating that she was from Catholic Charities in Des Moines, and having Jill declare that there was only one reason why she would be calling.

The second event was this phone call with Robert Stewart. In Kim's experience, many times, a man has been unsure of the request or denied paternity, but to have him do so and then immediately turn around and ask how her client was doing . . . was she happy, married, a mother? *That* was a first!

This of course was an interesting turn in the conversation, but it was obviously enough in my mind as well as Kim's to confirm who my birth father was. I was able to achieve what I wanted to with this part of my search: verify his identity and find a few photographs of him. As an adopted person, I have always been somewhat obsessed with the distinctive features of some families whose members all look alike, so it was equally as intriguing to get to see my physical similarities to my birth mother as well as my birth father.

In reading about or hearing others' stories about adoption, you rarely hear it from the birth father's perspective. When I contemplate what it must feel like to be the father of a baby given up for adoption, the only scenario that I was directly involved in was one in which the couple did not stay together and went on to marry someone else and begin their own families. So many times, we hear about the heartache and sense of loss that the birth mother experiences, but this cannot be easy on the father either. If indeed you have kept this baby a secret as you move on in life, there must be some sense of loss as well as that little voice in your head that pops up on occasion. What if my wife finds out? Why did I not tell her about this back when we were dating? The fear of having your wife, children, and grandchildren, who knew nothing about this child born out of wedlock, find out about their existence several decades later . . . this shrouded secret, it seems, could have the potential to possibly destroy a family. Hopefully that scenario doesn't happen often, but I can certainly understand the risk involved.

Acknowledgment of his part in the lineage of my existence would have been a bonus, but I already knew the truth. Thus, I was thankful to close that chapter of my search and still know that I had the best father a girl could ever ask for in Chuck Linn. I thank God every day for the precious fifty-three years that I got to have him in my life.

CHAPTER 9

Loss and Revelation

Dad's passing on Thanksgiving morning of 2012 was very painful. I had just left Fort Smith with our middle daughter Carolyn; we had driven to Fort Smith five days before Thanksgiving break to spend lots of time in the nursing home with Dad. We did not realize until we were there for a few days that his death was so imminent.

Dad had to move from my parents' home to a nursing home just a few days before Carolyn and I arrived for our visit. He spent the majority of his last nine days lying in the bed there, which the nurses had lowered close to the floor as he had been falling a lot. On my last night before we were driving home, I was alone with him; he had been quite agitated and unable to get comfortable, typical of an advanced dementia patient in the early evening hours. I did everything that Dad requested to attempt to get him relaxed, and after a few hours of sparring with himself, he finally laid his head softly on his pillow and dozed off.

About five minutes later, although I didn't immediately understand what was going on, my dad had a visit from Jesus himself I was blessed to witness. His eyes were closed and suddenly his fists were clenched and he appeared to be in the company of more than just me. My parents instilled a deep faith in me, and it's that faith that guided me through this difficult time. It's also that faith that told me that my dad was communicating with entities beyond what we know on earth. His shoulders dropped and curled inward; his body shook while he continued to have a discussion with someone who was part of Dad's reality but not mine. His lips were moving but there was nothing audible. When his lips were not moving, he appeared to be listening with his eyes closed. After roughly three to four minutes, he opened his eyes, looking forward, and then turned to look at me, realizing he wasn't alone. Then I asked him what the heck had just happened.

"Kathe," Dad declared while staring *through* my eyes, "it's my time."

Let me tell you, I've never had anyone look straight through me like he did at that moment. If you have ever been in the presence of a loved one about to pass over, maybe you understand what I'm talking about.

Of course, after being there and witnessing how much he had declined in just days, I knew the end couldn't be too far away and I thanked God that we had chosen to come visit during that time. But why was he declaring this right now?

Hoping that I was choosing the right words, I asked, "Dad, how could you possibly know?"

"Because my Lord just told me so."

My dad was a deeply spiritual man, his faith only growing as he aged. However, I had never heard him use that specific terminology when referring to Jesus. It was always "Jesus" or "God." When he said, "my Lord," I realized that this was coming from a different place and that his imminent passing was very real. It was almost as if he expressed the name that way to make sure that I was really paying attention.

When the last word of that sentence came out of his mouth, I broke down in hysterical tears, dropping my arms and head onto his chest. I suddenly became aware that the door to his room, just four feet away from us, was wide open and that my sobbing was attracting attention. I attempted to contain myself so more people wouldn't show up at the door.

"Dad . . . how incredible that He came to tell you! What does He look like?"

He turned his head again (the movement actually seemed rather mechanical) and looked straight at me. At this point, I was expecting a glorious description of white linen garments, flowing brown locks, and bright white light with glistening sparkles to come out of his mouth. Instead, I got . . .

"Kathe, are you making fun of me?"

Comic relief can be a beautiful thing. Suddenly my sobs of sorrow turned into contagious laughter. We were both sitting there splitting our sides right after one of the most poignant moments of both my dad's and my life. Of course, I wasn't making fun of him; I was just a living, breathing human being who happened to have never seen Jesus appear before me and wanted to know what he looked like! Clearly something very special had just happened to my dad, and I knew it was genuine. And there was that expression, "my Lord." Not in my dad's diction. Dad would be transitioning soon and his whole demeanor changed from that point on, from the usual ornery energy that is indicative of the last stages of dementia to a man at peace and ready to experience heaven. Who wouldn't be on board once they got the opportunity to discuss this event in the presence of Almighty God?

Not knowing *how* imminent this was, I gathered myself, grabbed my cell, and told Dad I'd be right back. I walked down the hall, then decided to keep walking to make sure I was out of his earshot. I quickly called my mom and told her she might want to get over here even though it was getting late; then I explained what had happened. I repeated the same call, this time with Jamie, who lived five minutes from Mom and Dad's. They both arrived shortly after, all of us awkwardly sitting around Dad's bed, not really knowing what to say except to tell him how much we loved him.

Dad fell asleep shortly after that and I just sat next to his bedside for hours. He awakened briefly at one point, and I again told him how deeply I loved him. There was no verbal response, but it registered in his eyes. Then he nodded off again. I just sat there, staring at him, so serene, while replaying so many scenes of our lives together. I knew without a doubt that this was it. I didn't want to go back to Mom and Dad's house to go to sleep because I knew that this was the last time I would see him alive.

Coming into this trip, Carolyn and I just thought it would be good to visit Dad and give him lots of love and support, being in a nursing home. We had no idea that he wouldn't still be around for another several months. How swiftly things changed. Carolyn and I would make the long drive back to Nashville the next morning just in time for Kat to fly home from college for the holiday break. We said goodbye to Mom, pulled out of their driveway, and started on to the highway that led us back to Nashville. That highway goes right past the exit to the nursing home that Dad was in, and I couldn't will myself to get off and go say goodbye one more time. To this day, I don't know why I kept going, and I cried for a long time about that. My heart was so broken that maybe the pain was at its ceiling, with nowhere else to go.

We arrived home on Wednesday night about the same time that Kat landed. The next morning, Thanksgiving, my mom called at 6:50 a.m.. Of course, she didn't have to tell me why she was calling.

❀ ❀ ❀

In the spring and summer of 2013, my relationship with my mom grew even closer with the loss of Dad. Mom had been diagnosed with COPD a number of years prior and she was at a point where she was on oxygen twenty-four hours a day. When Don and the girls left after my dad's funeral, I knew that I needed to stay with her for at least a week, possibly two. It was under the semblance of me helping her to get files, bills, insurance, and Dad's death records in order, but we both knew I needed to stay for emotional support. It was heartbreaking to leave her in Ft. Smith alone when it was time to go home. The round trip between her house and ours in Nashville was just under sixteen hours, but was always longer because Interstate 40 was in a constant state of construction. I begged her several times to move to Nashville, but she just felt that the city was too large. Nashville at that time, with suburbs, had a population of around 1.1 million, roughly double the size of Des Moines and its environs. It never occurred to me until the first time she mentioned the population of Nashville that Des Moines was the largest city that my parents had ever lived in.

After I was back home, Mom and I talked on the phone every night right before dinner, sometimes after dinner. With the frequency of our conversations, our talks could be as simple as Mom telling me about Shena, her Pomeranian, barking relentlessly at a visitor at the door, or what she was making for dinner that night. The point was to be in touch—somewhat simulating living close by—and to let her know that I missed Dad's presence just as much as she did.

During that spring and summer, I visited Mom as much as I could, probably once a month. Each time I was there, we would run whatever errands she needed to do and take care of projects she needed to take care of in the house. She never cared about feeding "those birds" in the backyard feeders until Dad was gone. It suddenly became all-important to keep those cardinals and chickadees fed, and as I loved my birds as much as Dad had, I was happy to oblige. Each time I came to town, we would also make a trip to the cemetery to visit Dad's grave.

My parents had elected a few years before Dad's passing to be buried in Fort Smith. This somewhat surprised my brother and me, as they had plots in Des Moines, where they had lived for over thirty years. They had retired to Hot Springs Village (HSV) in Arkansas back in 1984 due to their love of golf. HSV is a community loaded with golf courses in every direction you look. When sport was no longer in the picture due to their declining health, they decided to move to Fort Smith, two-and-a-half hours away, where my brother Jamie and his family lived. Mom and Dad had not lived in their new house in Fort Smith for even two years when Dad's health started to decline more rapidly. Before we knew it, we were trying to pick a cemetery in a city we weren't very familiar with to become my parents' final resting place.

Oak Cemetery in Fort Smith was an easy pick for our family. Established in the 1850s, this colorful cemetery is not only the final resting place for many lawmen and outlaws alike, but also is a beautiful piece of property sitting on over thirty acres, gently sloping from the center on both sides. There are over two hundred trees on the property, majestically protecting final resting places, including a beautiful variety of longstanding oaks. We chose a plot for Mom and Dad that faced the back entrance because it was near the top of the hill and overlooked a beautiful baseball field just across from the cemetery. We immediately loved how old the property was, with the resplendent black iron gates surrounding it, all in detail not found in current construction.

As the year progressed, each time I came to visit Mom I knew how much I wanted to tell her about my *accidental* discovery of my birth mother and subsequent connection with Marcia. Each time I came to visit, we would pick a day to run her errands and visit Dad's grave. Whenever we drove to the cemetery, I tried to gauge whether Mom was ready to take news of this magnitude. As far as she was concerned, I had never shown any interest in finding out anything about my birth parents, and she was correct . . . until recently. I had decided that I wanted to tell Mom at Dad's grave, where I felt his presence most clearly. I finally chose to tell her during my trip there in August, very close to what would have been my dad's eighty-fifth birthday.

Shortly after lunch, I drove Mom over to visit his grave and put some flowers out. I was surprised by how nervous I became during the fifteen-minute trip. I always tried to stay calm around Mom in those years; she needed to stay relaxed for the sake of her breathing. I took a deep breath at a stoplight and told myself that I hated keeping this secret from her and it was time to tell her what had happened.

As we wound up the road from the entrance, I looked at the beautiful red brick open building at the top of the hill, near the cemetery offices. This was where Dad's graveside services were rendered. I thought about that freezing cold day back in November, and all of the tears. That building always reminded me of the finality of his life really setting in. How I wished he was in the car with us for me to tell my story to both of them together.

I drove past the red brick structure and wound down to the gravel road that ran along the back side of Dad's grave. As we pulled up to Dad's spot, I parked the car and looked at Mom. She could tell that I had something very serious to say; her winsome, pale-blue eyes were searching my face for answers.

"Mom, I have something that I want to tell you about. I've wanted to tell you for over a year, but the timing just wasn't right with Dad's decline and passing."

As she was trying to respond to me, I broke down crying, or more accurately, sobbing. I couldn't believe that I couldn't hold it together long enough to tell her. I guess that I just didn't want to hurt her in any way, even though I couldn't keep this secret from her. She was my mother. She raised me. She came to stay with me each time one of our children was born, was there for every big event throughout my life. I definitely owed her the truth. I took a deep breath so that I could talk. My mom, of course, had no idea what I was about to convey to her . . . I imagine it was the furthest thing from her mind.

"Mom, since I wasn't able to tell both of you when Dad was alive, I purposely chose to tell you here at his grave. I've accidentally discovered who my birth mother was, and she is deceased. In the process I found out that I have a sister, one of the most wonderful human beings I've ever met. She is a really special person, and I can't believe I lived over five decades of my life without meeting her."

I nervously dove into telling her about how this all started with wanting to get more medical and social history for our daughters. Then about the mistake that was made when the original case manager had forgotten to eliminate my birth mother's last name on the two handwritten notes. However, I'm pretty sure that all that my mom heard at that juncture was that I had searched for and found my birth mother. I'm guessing she missed the word *accidentally* as well.

"Kathe, your dad and I always hoped that if you and your brother chose to find your birth parents, that you would do so after we had both passed."

Ouch.

She *had* only heard that I had searched for my birth mother.

Her comment threw me completely off guard, as she nor Dad had ever said anything about this to either Jamie or me previously. Thinking back on it, I should have realized that as little as they talked about us being adopted—the obligatory answers when someone asked about us being adopted, the actual stories of our adoptions—that talking about Jamie's and my four birth parents would be less than appealing for my mom and dad.

I had told Jamie about my birth mother journey and finding Marcia shortly after I first talked to my sister. I was curious about how he felt—if he might want to find out anything about his biological family. He knew where he could start; his file was sitting in the same place mine was at Catholic Charities in Des Moines. It seemed to me that he was not the least bit interested in pursuing any of the information, but I quickly reminded myself that I *thought* that that was how I felt too until that name wasn't whited out.

As important as it was for me to be honest with my mom about this, it was equally vital to me to make sure that she understood how all of this came about. Therefore, while we sat in her car next to my dad's grave, I started from the beginning and clearly laid out why I had wanted to do this for Lauren, Carolyn, and Kat.

I also explained that since the accident of leaving my birth mother's name on the letters was such an egregious mistake, I definitely felt like there was divine intervention involved. That wasn't a common error from an experienced social worker in that field.

In my heart, I had believed that I just wanted background for our daughters' health, as well as any social information that might be in my file. Had the last name not appeared, I never would have realized how I really felt about finding out. I wanted my mom, the woman sitting next to me who had raised me, loved me, loved my husband, and loved my children, to understand this fact: I had not known for 99 percent of my life if my birth mother was still living. However, if she was, I felt the duty to tell her that in choosing to put me up for adoption, she had done the right thing. I had been blessed with two incredible parents, a family that I loved dearly, and a great upbringing.

Mom sat patiently and listened while I explained the whole story. I could tell that she knew all of my words were sincere and that my intentions were honest. She leaned over from the passenger seat with her arms extended and we shared a prolonged embrace. We both smiled because we both knew how dearly I loved the woman who raised me. When we released our hug, I had no idea what was about to come out of her mouth.

"Let's go put those flowers on your dad's grave!" she affirmed.

An enormous sense of relief flooded my entire being. It was a rocky start to a tough discussion, but I felt that it had ended gracefully.

CHAPTER 10

Arizona Bound

A fter our initial visit at the beach, Marcia and I knew we needed to plan regular trips to continue to get to know each other. Living on opposite ends of the country, too much time would pass in between our chances to see each other unless we were deliberate about it. A year and a half after learning about each other and making that first phone call, it was time for me to meet the rest of her family, stay at her house in Phoenix, and get to know the place where she had lived for the majority of her life. The perfect opportunity presented itself with her upcoming landmark birthday.

Although Marcia's birthday was on February 1, the celebration of her fiftieth birthday was set for January 25, 2014. She had invited me to come to Phoenix for the first time to be a part of the events. I had some conflicts on my calendar but then realized how vacuous of me it would be to miss this opportunity. I took care of my schedule and promptly booked my flights. As I've admitted, I'm not the best when it comes to flying and turbulence. In my mind, a four-hour flight provides plenty of opportunity for bumps in the sky. My unbridled anticipation of seeing Marcia again and the chance to meet her family was mixed with my usual angst before flying, but once I was finally on the ground in Phoenix, I couldn't wait for the long weekend ahead.

I arrived at night and the ride from the airport was about forty-five minutes. By the time we got to the house, it was time for a quick tour and then off to bed. When Marcia showed me which bedroom I'd be sleeping in, she remembered that there was lots of memorabilia about our mother tucked under that bed. She pulled out a few of the photo albums and a quilt bought in Clinton that featured landmarks from DeWitt County, Illinois, which had belonged to Margaret. She asked me if I would like to have the quilt, and of course I was thrilled to have it.

Marcia went off to bed while I was perusing yet another album. There was so much information to look through—all just tucked neatly under that bed—that I stayed up way too late enjoying much of it. I could palpably feel my birth mother's presence, smiling down upon me as I exhumed page after page of her beautiful life. It was the first time I had ever felt her presence, as far as I could recall. That led me to wonder . . . was that because I'd never looked for it before?

The next night, Saturday, would be the night of the party at a clubhouse not far from their home. Marcia and I got up, went for a walk, and then drove over to the clubhouse to set some things up. While we were putting things out, we talked about who was going to be there. I was most excited about meeting all four of my sister's children during the same weekend: Chris, Michael, Caitie, and Megan. Many of their friends who were coming knew that I would be there. However, Marcia told me that she purposely did not tell some of her best friends who grew up with her and had known Margaret for most of their lives. As I resembled my birth mother so much, she wanted to see their reaction when they saw me for the first time. They knew that I had been invited, but last they heard, I probably wouldn't be able to make it. That night would be the first one of several where people looked at me as if I were a ghost.

I stood at Marcia's party that night, meeting one wonderful friend or family member after another. I remember when the party was approaching almost two hours underway, I noticed I hadn't even moved five feet from where I had initially been standing. Everyone I saw both upon my arrival on Friday and throughout Saturday I had obviously never met before, and what an incredibly warm and welcoming community they were. The reactions when most of them met me would have been fun to freeze in time. The looks of astonishment and comments about how it was indisputable who my birth mother was made for a great ice breaker while meeting so many new acquaintances.

The evening's highlight was Marcia and Mike standing up front and thanking everyone for coming, saying a prayer, and then Marcia singing. I was shocked and in great admiration of how beautiful her voice was. She had been working hard taking voice lessons, and it was clearly evident. I cannot carry much of a tune at all, so I was very impressed that someone who shared my DNA could belt it out so exquisitely!

It was such a blessing to be able to make my first trip to Marcia's home to be there for her fiftieth birthday celebration. The added bonus was a trip to Sedona. I felt so fortunate to have a sister who was thoughtful enough to offer to drive me almost two hours north of their home in Phoenix to visit my birth mother's grave for the first time.

We took pictures together in her den right before we got ready to drive up there. I caught a glimpse of myself in the mirror and thought, "This is the person who is fifty-four years old and is going to be sitting next to the physical resting place of her birth mother for the first time since birth, almost five-and-a-half decades later!" By that point, I was hoping that there would be some sort of spiritual connection when I was at her grave as well. I had no idea what to expect once I got to her grave, but I certainly hoped that I would at least feel Marti's presence. You know that feeling that you get when you're thinking of your grandmother who passed long ago, because it's her birthday and you still miss her so much? Or that sense when you visit your father's grave by yourself and are talking to him, telling him how much you will always love him, then suddenly you don't feel so alone? I just couldn't imagine that, being right there at the cemetery where Marti was buried, I wouldn't feel something.

We took off for the drive and I felt myself bursting with anticipation. The terrain along the highways fascinated me. Desert all around us, magnificent saguaro cacti jutting toward the sun, thriving in their home with little or no water. Some foothills, parts very flat, yet all very hot and dry even though it was the end of January. Back in Nashville it was the usual January weather, overcast and about forty degrees; such a huge contrast. We were close to the south side of Sedona and highway 89A took a curve and suddenly the most breathtaking sandstone monoliths appeared before us as we headed toward our destination. The beauty of the gigantic rock sculptures, cut over centuries with brilliant stripes of orange, red, pink, and even lavender, was beyond description. I was thankful that I wasn't driving, because I couldn't stop staring at their magnificent artistry, which only intensified as we drove closer.

As we rode into town, Marcia explained to me that many of these stone giants had names, such as Bell Rock, Cathedral Rock, and even Snoopy Rock. The outline of the top of the latter butte looked exactly like my favorite cartoon character when he laid on the top of his doghouse during so many decades of Peanuts comic strips. There were so many stunning buttes and views as we arrived that I wondered how people who came to Sedona decided where to go first and how to fit it all in.

Our agenda, of course, was different than most visitors'. Our priority was to go visit our mother's grave, where she was buried next to Marcia's father. But first we trekked to the Chapel of the Holy Cross, a stunning Catholic church that was built into the elevations of Sedona.

As we drove up to park on the road at the base of the chapel, I was once again in awe of another Sedona wonder. I had done some research on this chapel before we left to drive to Sedona. A local rancher and sculptor, Marguerite Brunswick Staude, had commissioned this stunning piece of architecture back in the 1950s. The chapel was completed in 1956, at a cost that seems miniscule today when one considers the difficulty of securing the structure into the side of the mountain. The total cost of the project was three hundred thousand dollars. I'm sure that if it were built today, it would draw a price tag twenty times that amount.

Marcia told me as we entered the church that our mother had left her Catholic faith many years before. When she became sick and was deciding where she wanted to be buried, she knew that it would be in Sedona, because she had loved the area so much ever since she had first visited. Then Marcia went on to tell me that there was something very special about this chapel for Margaret. She came back to the Chapel of the Holy Cross to make peace with the faith she was born into shortly before she left our earthly world. I felt such an incredible, tranquil energy standing in this amazing place of worship, right where my birth mother had made restitution with a major part of her spiritual life. Now I was ready to visit her final resting place.

Sedona Community Cemetery sits gently on a gradual hill on Pine Drive off Highway 179. Marcia brought a map of the cemetery from home just in case, because it had been years since she had been there. My birth mother's period of illness and death was one of the most painful times in Marcia's life. Not only had she lost her mother to cancer in the end of December 2002, but then her father passed from lung cancer less than three months later. Even though it had been over ten years since their passing, I could see as we were driving up the hill that this was opening up a very deep wound for my sister. I was immensely grateful—really beyond words—for her making this trip for me to witness Margaret's grave. She parked the car and walked me up to the site. Marcia was trying to hold back her tears, but as soon as we stood and looked down at the granite marker bearing our mother's name, Marcia began to cry softly and excused herself to walk down the hill. She told me to take all the time that I needed, which was beyond solicitous of her considering the feelings this had conjured up for her.

I sat down right next to the headstone and placed my hand where her first name was engraved. The stone was small and simple, flecks of gray dancing around her chiseled name as well as her husband Bob's name. I immediately felt an intense energy emanating from the granite. This made me think about what little I had heard about Sedona and its vortices—areas of concentrated energy coming up from the earth. Sedona was well known for four of them in particular, located at Cathedral Rock, Airport Mesa, Bell Rock, and Boynton Canyon. I wasn't sitting on top of any of these, but I noted that Cathedral Rock, one of the named breathtaking buttes, was about five minutes away. Why was I feeling this intense energy? Was it Sedona in general, or were my birth mother and I trying to find a way to connect? As out there as that may sound, something seemed to be happening. As I sat there next to her marker, I wished that I had researched this vortex phenomenon a lot more.

I looked down the hill and saw that Marcia had stopped about twenty feet away. It appeared that she was in prayer. I, too, was praying, but was just asking for some sort of connection with Marti while we were there in this breathtaking cemetery. I had missed the opportunity to tell Margaret in person how thankful I was for my life and her directive. Now was the time to attempt to communicate with her in another dimension.

I took several deep breaths to still my mind to receive anything. I tried to stay calm and meditate for a few minutes before instigating my request.

"If you are here with me right now, I would love to know. I of course cannot remember being with you at my birth, but I feel like we are together again for the first time since that day over five decades ago. I thank you with a profoundness that lacks words. I know what you did caused you great pain, but it's important for you to know that I feel that you did the right thing. My life has been incredible, with parents that have loved me unconditionally every moment along the way. Please find peace in these words."

I was prepared and knew that I was going to visit her grave to thank her, yet the way the words flowed from me once I was there with my hand on her gravestone surprised me.

"I have come a long distance to visit you and it would give me immense joy if you could give me a sign that you are here with us now."

As I was reaching out to her, the brilliant blue of two small, stunning birds that I had never seen before caught my eye. They were flitting around the cemetery and hopping from one juniper tree to another. Desperate for a sign, I grabbed my phone to figure out what these stunning feathered creatures might be and found that they were either mountain bluebirds or, more likely, western bluebirds, since they were at a higher elevation. As grateful as I was for their sighting, I realized quickly that this was not the sign that I was hoping for, as this bird was fairly common in this area, just new to me. I sat in silence for several more minutes with my hand on her marker. I finally let go of my impatience and felt a vast sense of peace.

I'm not sure how long after I got to that place of calm that I heard the most beautiful sound of simple bells nearby, just two or three times. To me they sounded like church bells, but the sound seemed way too close, considering there were no buildings anywhere near us. I got up and looked around to see if maybe there was a church nearby that was obscured from my view by so much vegetation. All that I could see were dozens of peaceful graves surrounded by trees and grass that blanketed the red, sandy soil. Also, since it was a weekday, I thought that maybe I was hearing noon church bells, even though the sound seemed much closer. I looked at my watch. It was 2:37 in the afternoon.

I jumped up from where I'd been sitting and walked down to my sister, whom I was thankful to see was much calmer by this point.

"Marcia, did you hear those bells ringing a minute ago?"

My sister looked at me, a bit confused. "What bells?"

"Any bells!"

"No, why? It's so quiet."

I smiled at my sister, then silently thanked my birth mother for finding a way to break through. I loved that, in that moment, I felt her presence next to the two of us. When I asked if she was there, I truly felt that she was.

My first trip to Phoenix and Sedona was beyond what I could have imagined. I loved that I was able to be at my sister's fiftieth birthday party and have the opportunity to meet many people she had grown up with that were very dear to her heart, both friends and family. Add to that what happened that afternoon in the most beautiful cemetery I'd ever stood in, and I felt blessed beyond words.

CHAPTER 11

Maurer Territory

L ess than four months after Marcia's fiftieth birthday and my first trip to her home in
Phoenix, served with a magical side dish of
Sedona, Marcia and her two youngest children, Caitie
and Megan, flew into Nashville to see our home and meet
my family for the first time. It was so much fun to show
them around town and the outskirts. The contrast of the
desert, saguaro cacti, and tiny quail of Phoenix with the
verdant foothills, horse farms, and deer of Nashville was
amazing to both of us.

Our plan was to spend a few days in Nashville and
Franklin and then drive to Clinton, Illinois, where
Margaret was born and raised and where many of her

relatives grew up. There were still family members that lived there, and Marcia was taking me there to meet them for the first time. Marcia had booked a room for us at the most interesting little hotel, called The Sunset Inn and Suites. Their lodging was a far cry from the mundane national and international hotel chains that blanket America. Although "regular rooms" were available, this locally-owned hotel had theme-based suites, and a dozen of them to choose from. You could go for a weekend in Arabia, swim under the sea, enjoy a space odyssey, or hang out in a rainforest, to name a few of their creative designs. Since it was my first visit to Clinton, the owners were kind enough to give us a tour of a number of the fantasy suites midday, in between visitors.

The weekend was full of plans and meeting new faces. I was most excited to meet my cousin Jill, the one who had walked into her dad Duane's house that day back in 2012, right when Kim Laube was calling from Catholic Charities in Des Moines. To this day, I wonder how long it would have taken to find my sister, if ever, had that divine timing not been in place. I will always be grateful to Jill for picking up that landline.

Once we had checked in, one of our first stops was at Uncle Duane's house. Rita (Margaret's younger sister) and Duane had been married since they were very young and had lived in this same welcoming house with a sprawling lawn and lofty trees for decades. Duane was so kind and receptive to this new relative appearing in Clinton for the first time. He was one of many people that weekend who would look at me for seconds longer than a normal glance, as if they were seeing an apparition, just as had happened at Marcia's birthday party months earlier. After the first half-dozen times, I just got used to it!

Marcia took me on a tour of this pretty and quaint town after leaving Duane's house. In a town of approximately seven thousand residents and only three to four square miles, much of it had touched the life of my birth mother. We drove from Duane's house to Woodlawn Cemetery, where Marcia showed me the graves of several family members, including Mom Maurer, my maternal birth grandmother, as well as Rita, Duane's wife and Margaret's sister. I was so touched when I found out that Duane went for a walk each morning after his beloved passed, ambling from his house to Rita's grave at Woodlawn and back, regardless of the weather. He apparently made the journey even in rain and snow, using his daily exercise to connect with all of their precious years together.

From there, Marcia took me by the house where our mother had grown up. As we sat in the car in front of the house, I found myself straining to look at the backyard, the location where so many pictures that

Marcia had sent to me were taken. Some were just of Margaret; many were of her with one or more of her family members. There were pictures from holidays and a picture of Margaret standing proudly next to her new bike with her older brother looking on. My favorite of all of them was of a smiling Margaret holding an apparently-coveted doll, with Rita standing next to her, scowling with her arms crossed so tightly, it made you wonder if she could breathe. I envisioned the two of them still standing in that yard as I gazed beyond the side of the house.

That evening, we met all of Duane's family that was still in town at a local favorite bar and grill. It was a great place to meet loved ones and just catch up, or in my case, meet a whole lot of family at once! I thought that it might be overwhelming to meet so many relatives at once, but it couldn't have been easier. Cousins, nephews, and nieces alike—all were more than welcoming and gave me the opportunity to get to know each one of them. Being raised in Des Moines, I often heard the term "salt of the earth" used to describe many people from the Midwest. This is how I felt sitting at this long table with most of the Harrises and Martins. I was proud to finally call them family. I was especially thankful for meeting my cousin who was closest to me in age, Doug Harris, Duane and Rita's middle child. It turned out that this was the first and only time that I would get to spend time with him, sitting right across the table from me. He left this earthly realm way too soon at the age of fifty-seven, three years later.

The following day, Marcia took me over to meet Bill and Elaine Smith. Bill had remarried after losing his wife Mary Anne to cancer. Mary Anne was Margaret's oldest sibling. On the way to their beautiful home, Marcia showed me where our mother used to ride her cherished horse. As we walked up the brick walkway to their house, I saw Bill sitting in his wheelchair with Elaine standing behind him, both looking out the front window. After meeting upon entering, Elaine told me that when they came to the window, they thought they saw a resurrected Margaret walking toward them with her daughter Marcia. There I was—the ghost again—but I didn't mind in the least.

Bill had been suffering from what I remember was a type of dementia for several years, so much of our discussion during the visit was with Elaine. Bill had been an attorney in Clinton for forty-six years before retiring. Marcia had heard from Aunt Rita that Margaret had come to him when she was pregnant with me, needing some legal advice and help dealing with my birth father. Therefore, we knew that he was in the very intimate circle of people my birth mother had trusted with her secret. We were tempted to ask Bill about the details of this legal issue he had helped my birth mother out with so many years ago, but it didn't feel the least bit appropriate seeing him in a wheelchair, just an eyelash away from ninety years old.

Marcia and I had run into enough dead ends when trying to get the whole story about our mom's pregnancy. There were so few people that were in the know about Marti's pregnancy, and most of them had passed away. Having Bill right in front of us, knowing that he knew at the very *least* a lot more than we did, had me chomping at the bit to pick his brain. It was hard to look at him and not at least try to talk with him about it, but I resisted the temptation out of respect. As little as Bill did seem to recall, one thing was sure from our observation . . . he remembered Margaret!

That evening, our last night in town, Uncle Duane invited Marcia, the girls, and me to be the guests of honor at an outdoor cookout at his home. As many of his neighbors had lived near him for decades, the closest of those friends were invited, as well as Jill (his youngest) and her husband Chad, Stan (his oldest) and his wife Pam, and many others. Before the friends arrived, Duane and Pam directed us into the dining room, where they had laid out several family pictures, which included photos of Margaret with other family members. It was fascinating to look at all these images for the first time, and once again, I was overwhelmed with gratitude for the chance meeting of so many relatives that I could easily have never known.

Duane showed me a tiny painting of a male cardinal in a round frame, and told me that Margaret had given it to Rita and him decades ago. I then divulged that I have been a bird geek my whole life, starting with the cardinals that used to dine at my grandfather Linn's feeders in the mountains of North Carolina. Duane couldn't wait to take the painting off the wall and give it to me. When I arrived back in Nashville after that trip, I hung it on the wall coming in from our garage to our house, so every time I come home it reminds me of Margaret, not to mention Duane.

Before the rest of the guests arrived, we went out to the backyard and took some family pictures. As I stood in this part of the yard for the first time, I admired Duane's splendid gardens. I realized that this was a man who didn't sit still for long. He seemed to always be doing something, which was amazing for someone approaching eighty years old, starting with that walk each day. I decided I want to be just like my new uncle when I grow up—always on the move with projects to spare at eighty.

The barbeque was planned for the perfect night. The weather was ideal for a May evening in Illinois, and at one point I just sat back in a chair and watched all the conversation and love spreading throughout the front yard and the driveway. The garage was open, where a group of men, including Duane, were sitting on folding chairs, reminiscing while having a beer or two. What a wonderful way to wrap up my first trip with my sister to Clinton, Illinois, birthplace and childhood home of Margaret Maurer.

CHAPTER 12

Synchropregnic-ity

September 1987 was an extremely exciting time in my husband Don's and my life. I was pregnant with our first child and due on September 24, Don's twenty-ninth birthday. I was thankful to have survived the sweltering Texas summer in Dallas during my third trimester and was looking forward to having our precious little girl or boy out of my now-behemoth body.

On the morning of September 9, I took our Brittany spaniel, Rex, out for our usual walk and began to have what I thought were just more Braxton-Hicks contractions. I had been experiencing these false labor signs for a few weeks now, but as was indicative of Braxton-Hicks, there had been no regular pattern of contractions up until this point. I certainly didn't find them to be particularly painful, so at first, I thought nothing of it. After all, I wasn't due for more than two weeks, and my friends who had given birth before me had all made it to their due dates, most of them going past them.

As we continued to walk down the street, I noticed that this tightening was now coming in regular intervals. This was not the irregular timing of pains that I had felt previously. Instead of walking our full usual path, I went down to the end of the block that we were on and turned Rex around for home. About ten to fifteen minutes later we were back in the house, and I had my obstetrician's nurse on the phone.

"This is Kathe Caire. I'm probably overreacting because my due date is fifteen days away. I've been experiencing what I'm thinking is just Braxton-Hicks, but they seem somewhat stronger than before, so just to be safe I thought I had better call you. I need to finish walking my dog but thought I'd better check in . . ."

"How far apart are your contractions?"

"I've been timing them for maybe the last half hour, and they seem to be five to seven minutes apart."

I remember the nurse being quite surprised by this information, mainly because I had continued walking my dog for a while before thinking that I had better double-check. (Yep...ignorant first-time mother, thinking she knows what she's doing.)

"Kathe, I have no idea how you are out walking your dog like that, but your walk is over for the day. You need to get down to the hospital right now."

Fortunately, my bag was already packed; I decided some time back that I would have my hospital bag ready to go at least three weeks before my due date. I thanked my nurse, hung up the phone, and called Don. It was a Wednesday morning, so he was already at work, but he was able to rush home quickly.

Our first home was a darling two-bedroom, one-bath Tudor with stained glass windows, built in 1926. We lived in an area called the "M Streets," where most of the driveways were single-lane drives, most of them without garages. We had a garage in the back of the lot that was barely hanging on and certainly not safe for housing cars. Thus, we always parked both cars in the driveway. Don was in the house less than five minutes before we'd given Rex his food and water and made a beeline out the front door to his car, both of us pretty impressed with how quickly we were on our way to the hospital. We jumped in Don's big old Thunderbird and he put the key in the ignition.

Nothing.

I was now in active labor and the two of us were sitting in a car with a very dead battery. We must have been quite a sight with me and my huge belly getting out of the car and going around to get in the driver's seat while Don pushed the T-bird down the driveway. Fortunately, we were laughing instead of panicking; it was just such bad timing! Once his car was backed up enough, we got in my car that was parked in front of it and backed up around the Thunderbird through our front yard. Then off we went to Baylor Hospital!

My labor down at the hospital was not your typical first birthing process. I ended up being in labor for almost eighteen hours, based on when the doctor and nurses said it started. Although that sounds long, it wasn't really very painful until I was in transition. Even then, I was trying my best to finish a needlepoint wedding pillow that I was making as a gift for one of my best friends, Karin, and her soon-to-be husband. Our doctor thought that seeing me needlepoint even during transition was entertaining enough to bring in two or three residents to witness it personally. That was the first time it registered with me that having a baby is not a very private experience.

As it got to be the middle of the evening, I realized that we might be having a baby on *my* birthday instead of the due date of Don's birthday. My first thought was,

This is so cool. There are 365 days in a year and I'm going to have a baby born on the same day as me! Then came the part where my mind just kept churning. *If we have a child born on my birthday, what will our subsequent children think? Will they think he or she is special? That we favor that child over the others?* (Yes, I am very aware of my tendency to overanalyze.) In a matter of hours, it would be my twenty-eighth birthday, so whatever happened, would happen. As it turned out, our obstetrician delivered our first daughter, Lauren, at 11:56 p.m. that night, September 9, 1987, a few minutes shy of my birthday.

Margaret's Journal

September 1987—Phoenix, AZ

I had been working in Labor and Delivery at Thunderbird Hospital for about three years when one of the biggest events of our lives occurred; the birth of our first grandchild. Since I was employed at the hospital in L&D, I was able to help Marcia, who was now over nine months pregnant, with her labor and the birth. Already six days past her due date, Marcia was certainly ready for this event to happen. She had labored for hours at home, and I coached her some on her breathing as she hung onto "Budget," a teddy bear, as a focal point. She was completely dilated and ready for delivery upon arrival at the hospital. I was so excited when I heard that I had trouble getting my scrubs on! There was no time for the obstetrician to deliver the baby, so the emergency room doctor did the honors. When I went into the hall to tell my husband Bob, "It's a boy," he began to cry. It was such a poignant moment for all of us and a high point in our lives. Marcia and Jeff named him Christopher James, born on September 21, 1987 at 11:07 p.m. Our first grandchild! He was a beautiful little boy; even the nursery staff said so. It was like reliving the thrill of the birth of our own child.

❀ ❀ ❀

As Margaret stated in her journal, she became a grandmother for the first time. In yet another event of synchronicity, it turns out that she became a grandmother twice that month in 1987—once in every sense of the word "grandmother," and once because of shared DNA. While she had no way of knowing this transpired, Marcia and I were still in awe to realize that we had given birth to our firstborns so close to each other. My Lauren was born six days before Marcia's due date, Christopher born six days after. The odds of that happening were amazing to me, and even after Marcia and I had met it took us awhile to put it together. Maybe it was just another little divine sign that we were connected, regardless of how many years it took us to find out.

CHAPTER 13

Facing the Unknown

E ver since I discovered that my birth mother
had a name and was a living, breathing person,
I have often wondered what exactly transpired
in the months leading up to my birth and adoption, what
it must have been like for her, what she felt, how she
handled it, and ultimately, what she regretted. Although
many details in this chapter come from Marti's journals
and knowledge passed on to me by my sister, her pregnancy with me and subsequent birth were conspicuously
absent from her chronicles. We do know that she thought

about it enough to share it with Marcia that one day in 1989. After going through this surprising and ultimately rewarding experience of discovery, I allowed myself to wonder about Margaret's inner life during that time, just so I could imagine for myself what it might have been like to be in her shoes.

Below is my version—with some creative license—of what an unwed girl named Margaret, from Clinton, Illinois, with dreams of being a lifelong nurse, might have gone through in 1959. Though what follows is fiction, with history interspersed, the truth of the matter remains: Margaret Maurer was a perfectly human person, with a difficult choice to make, and I am eternally grateful to her for that choice.

For all that she went through and all that she did for me, this chapter is dedicated to my birth mother, who gave me life, then gave me the greatest gift in my adoptive parents.

Margaret (Marti) Maurer

Spring of 1959

I don't know how this could have happened to me. Well, truth be known, I know exactly how it happened to me.

I loved my time in Champaign at Mercy Hospital School of Nursing. I was born and raised in a small town in Illinois called Clinton. I had lived there my whole life until I moved less than an hour away to go to nursing school. My nursing cohorts, many of whom became dear friends of mine, were at my side as we worked through rotations and went to classes, all striving to make it to the finish line. Debbie Bates, who I affectionately called "Bato," and Maureen Hagan, "Mo," were my roommates almost the entire time.

During what little time we had for fun, Bato, Mo, myself, and a small group of other nursing students would make our way over to the University of Illinois campus to a favorite hangout, where we would meet lots of interesting guys that were at U of I or had graduated in recent years. On Friday nights, the bar had "Buckets of Suds" specials, which all of us loved to partake in because it made sense on our limited budgets—and boy was it fun! One Friday night, we decided to try a new place for us, recommended by some of our other nursing buddies. It was up the road a bit from Champaign, in a town called Rantoul. Another favorite hangout for many people our age, it was called Wings and was located on Chanute Air Force Base.

On one of those nights at Wings, I met a very handsome gentleman named Robert who, by the age of twenty-three, already owned a mobile home distribution business in a nearby town. He and I hit it off immediately. He was 6'3", and had dark, wavy hair and beautiful green eyes. He came over to our table and we talked for hours . . . not just small talk, but instead actually getting to know each other. By the time Mo, Bato, and I left that night, I was amazed at how enamored I was with Robert already. He had asked for my number, but he'd also had a few beers. I tried not to get my hopes up that he would call.

To my surprise and delight, he called me the next afternoon. We immediately began dating and saw each other whenever we had free time. When we had been going out for over six months, it seemed like it had only been a few weeks. Time with him was easy and flowing and he was a blast to be with. We enjoyed the same sports and we delighted in playing them together. He also taught me how to waterski and I taught him how to be a better tennis player. We loved packing big picnic lunches and trying out new parks to enjoy our fare. Even going to the movies, which we both revered, was an extra adventure because we both adored the old and the new.

If this all sounds a bit too idyllic, I soon found out that it was.

At first, I just thought that my period being late was nothing. With my crazy schedules all through nursing school and even at the hospital, erratic periods were nothing new. Then I got to the following month and once again . . . nothing. It wasn't long after that that I noticed my breasts were very tender, on and off throughout the day. This was definitely something that I didn't remember ever feeling previously. I suspected what was going on but was too terrified to tell anyone. In fact, it took me weeks to even mention it to Mo and Bato. They of course suggested that I tell Robert that I was pretty sure that I was pregnant. I decided that I wanted confirmation from a doctor first. Certainly not our family doctor in Clinton, because no matter what, I was not going to tell my parents. Whether I wanted to admit it or not, both of my parents put me on a pedestal. I couldn't bear to think about them looking at me and the shame it would bring.

I was fairly certain that both my mom and my dad thought I'd never made a poor choice in my life. Except, perhaps, for that time as a young child that I decided on a Saturday night to go see my dad at his car dealership. I just walked out the door without asking my mom and walked across town. With that exception (which I paid dearly for) I did feel like I had made pretty solid decisions all my life up to this point, and if my parents found out about this, who I was as their daughter would have a whole new slant in their eyes. I absolutely could not let them know if I turned out to be expecting. If I was, I was going to need some serious support from my sisters, Mary Anne and Rita.

Since home was about forty-five minutes away from Champaign, I decided it would be safe enough going to a doctor in Champaign just to stay away from Clinton. Clinton is just small enough that everyone knows each other, so even with doctor-patient privilege, staying away from home seemed wisest. Bato helped me to pick an OBGYN in Champaign that didn't know me from school or rotations. I made an appointment on a Tuesday afternoon during lunch, which probably wasn't the most brilliant decision. After leaving my urine sample and answering the doctor's questions, I left the office, hurried through the parking lot to my car, and as soon as I had unlocked the door and got in, I was crying hysterically. Although it would be at least a week before the results came back, I just *knew* by the way the doctor looked at me with each successive question that all indications made pregnancy an almost sure bet. In hindsight, I think that not telling Robert earlier that I suspected I might be pregnant made for a very desolate mindset that afternoon. Right there, in my car, I felt like I was completely and utterly alone, with absolutely no one to turn to.

When I got home later that evening, Mo and Bato could not have been more supportive. Friends just don't get any better than that. They talked me through where to go from that point and I made a commitment to myself to tell Robert the following week when the results came back, if indeed the test was positive. Of course, the wait was agonizing—my mind slowed time down like it was oozing through quicksand. My brain also started to play tricks on me; I felt as though my belly was stretching daily and that I was waking up every morning a few pounds heavier. I finally heard back from the OBGYN a little over a week later and my fears were confirmed: I was indeed with child.

During my lunch break that day, I called Robert and asked him to meet me after work. I was quite sure that he knew the news was not good by the audible quivering of my voice. I was extremely thankful that not only was he available to see me, but that he didn't start asking questions over the phone. More evidence that he might have suspected the news wasn't so favorable.

We had agreed to meet at a park not too far from the hospital shortly after my shift was over. I told him the second we laid eyes on each other, then burst into tears. He held me, and somehow I discerned that he had already guessed what this meeting was about. We sat there on a park bench for what seemed like several minutes in silence, although it was probably thirty seconds or so. Then he told me that he wasn't ready for marriage. Hardly what I needed right at that moment, but I guess he was just saying what was on his mind. I was just trying to deal with the stress of this baby being real; I hadn't gotten to the *future* part yet.

That night, I went home and cried a lot more. This time, at least I had the girls there to support me instead of when I sat alone in my car wailing after my appointment. I needed to have a plan to get through this and time was of the essence. The doctor guessed that I was already close to the end of my first trimester, and I wasn't sure if that surprised me or panicked me more. I had already figured out that I needed to move somewhere to hide during the end of my pregnancy; the question was where. I had relatives in different towns in Illinois besides Clinton, but when I considered my options, I felt like this was a time when being part of a huge, close family was not working in my favor. I felt pretty certain that if I sought refuge with one of my aunts or uncles and a job in the same town, the word would get back to Mom and Dad quite swiftly.

I needed time to make a plan, and moving away from central Illinois was scary. It was all I'd ever known, and up until I went to nursing school in Champaign, I'd always lived in tiny Clinton. This was the first time I'd put together a resume since I'd entered the working world, so I hit the ground running the next morning, trying to figure out the best way to present myself for a much-needed new job in a completely foreign city. For a few weeks, I thought about looking for a job in Chicago or Indianapolis and did some research comparing the two. However, when it came down to actually sending my resume, the size of those cities made me pause and rethink my options. Shortly after, Mo brought to my attention that I had a logical connection to Des Moines, Iowa.

The next Monday I went into my supervisor Linda's office and asked to set up a time for us to talk. I guess because of the inordinate stress that she read on my face, she invited me to sit down and discuss whatever it was immediately. I really loved this job and loved my coworkers. I could feel my eyes beginning to water before I even started to explain why I was sitting there (or rather . . . my fabricated excuse for why I was sitting there). I told her that I had lived in this part of central Illinois my entire life and that I felt like it was time to try somewhere new for a while. I could tell that I had caught her off guard; she clearly didn't see this coming. But truth be told, I hadn't seen it coming either. I told her that I had heard of other nurses transferring to different hospitals in the Mercy system and was wondering if she might know how to go about this.

Of course, I did not bring this up with Linda, but I had a connection that might be comfortable enough for me to start off somewhere new with a little help from my friends. Mo's parents were in Des Moines, where she had grown up. As we talked through things the week before, Mo mentioned that moving there and telling only her mom and dad might be a safe way for me to get started. She felt sure that they would even let me stay with them until I found my own apartment and procured a nursing job.

Linda shifted uncomfortably in her chair. Her pause made me think she was choosing her words carefully. "Marti, you are such an asset here and clearly love working with these mothers and babies. Are you sure about this?"

"Linda, I am pretty certain and have thought through this a lot." (Of course, *that* wasn't entirely true, but I was making my best attempt to sound calm and organized about this request, as if I'd thought about it for several months.) "I even think I know where I'd like to go. I know there is a Mercy Hospital in Des Moines. The city is midwestern like I am used to, but larger than Champaign and vastly bigger than Clinton. It's a decent distance from home and my family without being a really long drive. Could you make a call for me and if you feel I've been a good employee, please put in a nice recommendation about my abilities?"

"I will see what I can do. But I am really going to miss you. A lot."

Linda's honest expression about our close working relationship made me close to tearing up, but I knew I needed to stick with the intended dialogue. Thinking about how much I was going to miss her and our department might make me break down and start spewing a tell-all about my predicament.

"I will miss you and everyone here immensely," I insisted, probably *way* too robotically. "I just know that this is the right thing to do at this juncture in my career."

It took a little over a week for Linda to make contact with the appropriate people at Mercy in Des Moines, but she did me right. She must have given me a glowing recommendation and they must have needed more nurses in their OBGYN unit. The timing of my request seemed divinely orchestrated. Mercy had just opened a new obstetrical department in the south wing of the hospital there. When I spoke with Lisa in human resources, she seemed very eager to interview me and was already telling me extensively about the position available for me. By this point, Mo had already told her parents about the situation and they were more than happy to take me into their home while I interviewed and found a place of my own to live, at least through the end of my pregnancy.

Needless to say, I was very anxious to leave town as soon as possible, but nervous about how much unknown I was pushing myself into. Although my belly might not have been showing to others, I could feel the pressure on my waistband pushing out just a tiny bit further every morning when I got out of bed.

As stressful as my situation was, I was so grateful about the way things were falling into place. The panic that set in about getting out of town before my belly was discovered (by anyone remotely close to my parents) was relieved by the efficiency of finding a safe place to move to temporarily and a job at the other Mercy Hospital falling into place smoothly. I was offered an interview and had less than two weeks to get there. As now seemed par for the course, Linda was remarkably understanding about the timing of all of this as well. I explained to her that there was a nursing position available in Des Moines that could possibly be a great fit for me. When I told her that I had an interview, she kindly consented to my taking time off, sensing that this was it and I wasn't coming back.

The drive to Des Moines was five to six hours, depending on how many stops I made. I thanked Jesus for giving me a dad who was a car dealer. I had never driven by myself on any road trip even remotely this long, and Daddy always provided his children with a good deal on a safe used car. I knew I was going to need it, because I sure didn't need anything else to stress out about. I spent the weekend before the trip packing up my things while concurrently reminiscing and crying with Bato and Mo. They had been such immense pillars of support for me always—but especially through all of this—and now Mo's parents were going to continue to extend that backing. I hoped to get the job offer and find an apartment not too far from the hospital soon, but what a relief to have them there for me!

As unhappy as I was with Robert's reaction to our pregnancy news, I still knew that I loved him and should at least fill him in on my decision to move to Iowa. At least he could be relieved to know that his now-ex-girlfriend would be out of sight from all our friends and acquaintances during the very visible part of my pregnancy. To be honest, Robert seemed more upset than I expected him to be when I told him that I was moving to Des Moines. I explained to him that if I was driving that far, I was going to pack up my belongings and make sure that I got a job after my interview. If one didn't materialize, I'd find one at another hospital in that city!

Suddenly I had a flashback to what my mom had always told me about my character, even with events as young as nine months old. She said that I had always been tough and determined from the get-go. With precise clarity, I could certainly see that determination shining through right now. In such a situation, it could be so easy to give in to my hormones and just cry and give up, but I knew that I could make it through this. My mom was right about me. When I put my mind to something, I kept pressing on to make it happen!

As for Robert, around four or five months into us dating, I truly felt that he was the one—that we were soulmates, if such a thing existed. Judging by his words and actions, it is fair to say he was thinking the same way (that is, before our inopportune news came between the two of us). However, the moment that he said he wasn't ready for marriage, I knew that this wasn't just a matter of timing. Anyone who could bring that up so bluntly immediately after I hysterically relayed my difficult news was most likely not in it for the long run, as far as I could imagine.

Two days before I took off for Des Moines, Robert asked me out to dinner, I assumed just to say goodbye. He had already told me that he would help with my pregnancy expenses, as I had told him that I would be putting the baby up for adoption. Considering the finality of our discussions, imagine my surprise when I found out what our "goodbye" dinner was about. After we had finished our entrees, he got out of his chair, dropped one knee to the floor, and asked me to marry him! Arms thrust forward, both hands cradling a blue velvet box, now opened and revealing . . . what? An engagement ring that tempted me with security and a promise for all of my stresses to come to a screeching halt.

I couldn't believe what was happening . . . and immediately wondered why the somewhat sudden change of heart. Was he honestly afraid of losing me because I was moving, or was he trying to do the honorable thing before it was too late? I've never been one to make a scene in public, and I suddenly felt my cheeks, my neck, most probably my entire being turning red as I tried to secretly glance to my right, then slowly to my left. As I feared, due to my date being on one knee with a token of love stretched toward me, we unfortunately had the attention of every patron in the restaurant.

As baffled as I was considering his previous lack of emotional support, I quietly told him we should discuss this in private. The ride back to my apartment was silent enough to hear the crickets sing, but fortunately was only ten minutes long. There was an unnatural stillness that enveloped the car for most of the ride. This last-minute proposal made me think about what might have changed in his mind during the little over two months since I had shared our pregnancy news. Although his offer to marry me seemed genuine, it also felt forced. Although this is what I perceived, it may have simply been my own protection mechanism, since I'd already made my decision.

As he pulled up to my apartment, I gave him my answer, which he probably already knew. I felt a very bittersweet sense of relief as I jumped out of his car without waiting for him to come over and open my door.

❀ ❀ ❀

My trip to Des Moines was just as uneventful as I had prayed it would be. I arrived in the early evening while it was still light out. I was pleasantly surprised at how beautiful this city was. With it also being a Midwestern town, I expected it to look a lot like many of the small towns in Illinois that I had known while growing up. Conversely, Des Moines was very verdant this time of the year and had beautiful, rolling hills, and I loved the architecture in the old neighborhoods surrounding the Hagans' house. I had adored Mo's parents since the first time I met them, and I truly was in love with them as they met me at my car as soon as I drove up and both gave me huge, genuine hugs.

Before I could grab my bags, her mom whisked me inside, while Daddy Hagan took all of my bags and belongings up to their very comfortable guest room on the second floor. The smell of a pot roast that had probably been cooking for hours filled the whole house with a splendid aroma of love and hospitality. Momma Hagan showed me the way up to my temporary room and gave me some privacy before dinner to get comfortable. I felt so overwhelmed with love; it was such a dichotomy of emotions in such a short amount of time.

I suddenly got teary-eyed once again, but this time I was thinking of how desperately I missed my parents. My dad was always my hero, and my mom was my eternal rock. The fact that I had made it to Iowa safely and was about to embark on a new chapter in my life seemed so wrong to be happening without them as a part of it. They were there for me for everything. But, still, I couldn't bear the thought of letting them down. I imagined their faces repeatedly in my mind, pretending that I *had* told them, and seeing the sheer disappointment, not ever guessing that I would have made such a poor decision.

I knew just how heavily this not telling them was weighing on my mind when I actually had a long dream about it one night. In it, I had a significant baby bump, and I was in our house in Clinton and both Mom and Dad were home. For hours, I darted from one place to another where I could hide my protruding belly. Sitting at a chair, slid right up to the dining room table with my belly masked underneath, standing next to any corner where walls converged, talking to them with my midsection tucked on the other side. This seemed to go on for hours, and somehow, they never noticed.

Clearly, my predicament had me stressed during my sleeping hours as well. This was exemplary of the constant ups and downs I felt for almost seven months. One day I'd be strong and decide I was moving away and capable of doing it all on my own, the next I'd be distraught and missing not only my parents but everyone in my family. I don't know what I would have done if I didn't have my sisters and my best friends to talk to about this.

❀ ❀ ❀

My interview that Tuesday went beautifully. Cyd, the head nurse who I spent the most time with that day, was so kind and welcoming that I even decided to risk the whole truth. Before she had even offered me the job, I just blurted out why I had made this major decision to move to Des Moines on a moment's notice. As soon as it came out of my mouth, I couldn't believe I was confiding in this kind woman I had just met. The risk of what I was spilling was inordinate but just seemed right. There was just something about her.

As fate smiled upon me once again, she shared with me that this same situation had happened to her sister years ago and she had also gone away to have her baby. She said it seemed that no one knew except the few members of her family whom she had confided in and having the baby away from home relieved a tremendous amount of pressure for her sister. Cyd offered me

the position in OBGYN before I had left the building. She made sure to introduce me to others within
the group and even give me some interview time with
three potential coworkers. The fear of looking too eager
wasn't even on my radar at that point. I was really lik-
ing the people, the new wing of the hospital, and the
uplifting energy of the department. The terms of the
offer were even more favorable than I had hoped; I was
used to small-town salaries and not a lot of benefits.

I accepted emphatically after she asked if starting
the following Monday would be too soon. This would
give me time to spend a day looking at apartments with
the agent Daddy Hagan had recommended. Two days
later, I found the perfect little place that was ready for a
move-in. It was relatively close to Mercy and was cheap;
those two criteria were my chief priorities. The Hagans
helped me with my move, and it seemed like they
wouldn't let me pick up anything that weighed more
than eight ounces. Once my rather limited possessions
were in the apartment, I thanked them profusely and
promised to have them over for dinner soon. I closed
the door and collapsed on an old couch that was graciously lent to me by these two precious guardian angels.

It suddenly occurred to me that I was living by myself
for the first time in my entire life; in fact, I'd always had
a roommate or two, whether it was my sister, classmates
in nursing school, or a friend. It was oddly quiet but not

such a bad thing. I had moved to another state on my own, found an awesome job, and was now in my own apartment. As tired as I was by the end of each day, this new sense of autonomy felt inspiring and intoxicating.

For the next several months, work consumed my days. Despite me being a new employee, I felt like Cyd was looking out for me with the shifts she gave me week after week. I needed every minute of sleep that I had time for, and she knew it. She really was my only confidante at work during that period of time. I knew that once I was showing, obviously everyone around me would know that I was pregnant, but I asked Cyd to keep the details quiet and she graciously obliged. Any questions about my personal life from other coworkers were few and far between . . . and were always met with the shortest answers possible.

I knew from almost day one that I wanted to give the baby up for adoption. This clearly provided the best opportunity for the child's rearing and future, and the best possibility for me to get on with my life. Robert sent me a kind letter and some money about a month into my moving to Des Moines, but I had long since given up hope that our love for each other would survive this. I looked into what adoption agencies were servicing middle Iowa, and clearly the most logical one with my background and religious beliefs was Catholic Charities. I hoped in choosing that organization that I would be able to pick, or at least help pick, a wonderful Catholic couple to raise my baby. I had all the usual hopes and dreams for the best life for my child; those plans just didn't include me.

Outside of work, there were two women who, along with Cyd, sustained me and kept me going. This is why I was so thankful that I decided to contact Catholic Charities sooner rather than later. The first was Mrs. Loehr, who was the social worker assigned to my case since the first day that I called there. When I first picked up the phone to call the organization, my thoughts were constantly focused on, "What type of mother gives up her baby to someone else? What will these people think of me?" However, all it took was one conversation with Mrs. Loehr to settle me down and know that she was welcoming me with open arms. I had so many questions, concerns, and anxieties during the months that I worked with the adoption agency, and sometimes I felt like I was her only client . . . she was just that good to me.

Then there was the ethereal Sister Zita. Sister Mary Zita was born in Ireland but came to the US at only fifteen years of age to live on her uncle's farm northeast of Des Moines. Fortunately for central Iowa, she became a fixture of compassion and love at Mercy Hospital for decades. I first met Sister Zita during my second week of work there. I was busy checking on my babies when

Sister Zita met me in the hallway, introduced herself, and held my hand. There was something very special about her from that first moment. She didn't just hold my hand; she gently clasped both of her hands around mine, and it lasted much longer than the usual handshake. It was as if a cocoon had swaddled my cold and lonely hand (or were those hands coddling my heart?) to tell me that everything was going to be okay. I've always thought that she knew just by the pain in my eyes what was really going on.

Of course, it wasn't long after that I told her my *entire* story, starting with the first night that I met Robert. The love and support she gave me from that day forward was second to none, including through the birth and as I gave the baby up for adoption. She was my divine gift from God during those months.

From my work in obstetrics up to this point, it seemed that a number of the young mothers that I worked with would go past their due dates and deliver within a week or so after that. It probably wasn't the norm; I just remembered those cases much more clearly because the women were so uncomfortable by that point. As I was due on September 24, I was surprised when I felt the baby drop in late August. During my checkup that week I was also *not* surprised to find out that I had started to dilate, because my contractions were beginning to take on a regularity and intensity that were not present previously. When I first accepted my job and confided in Cyd over three months before, we had planned that I would take off the last week or two depending on how I was feeling. However, now that the finish line was nearing, I was more efficient and full of immense strength and energy. I might have worked twenty-four-hour shifts if I'd been allowed to, because I suddenly saw no end to my stamina.

On the morning of September 9, 1959, my water broke. All over Mercy Obstetrics's glistening clean hallway.

It honestly was not as painful as you would think, despite labor going on for over fourteen hours. Maybe I'd soaked up quite a bit of pain management in working with my delivering patients in my young career. At 12:48 a.m., September 10, 1959, I gave birth to a healthy baby girl with the same color hair as mine. She weighed six pounds, eight-and-a-half ounces and was nineteen inches long. She had angel kisses (my mom and grandma called them stork bites) on one eyelid, on her forehead and at the nape of her neck. I named her Mary Katherine.

I took my time in signing the legal documents for her adoption, maybe because I was in awe of actually being a mother. I'm still not sure what caused me to take days to sign the papers. I thought about calling Robert or simply writing him a letter, but as his communication with me during the pregnancy was spotty at best, I felt that he just wanted the whole predicament to go away, which quite frankly was just how I was thinking as well. Interacting with him, even on a limited basis, just added to the pain, so I chose to avoid the call altogether. I had no doubt that he would hear about it without me being the messenger.

On September 14, I signed my release of custody of Mary Katherine Maurer. She was transferred to the Christ Child Home in Des Moines the next day to be put up for adoption through Catholic Charities.

The simple signing of a few pieces of paper, and my daughter was no longer my daughter. The hardest part about making choices in general is that we don't get to know what would have been. After this day, I wouldn't know what happened to her, if her name changed, if she had my green eyes, if she was tall like her father, or stubborn like me. I wouldn't know what her life would be like, what her hobbies entailed, what she liked to eat, or wear, or say. I would not know what she thought of me, or even if she ever would. I could only hope that one day, she'd understand that the only gift I could truly give her was to be a part of a loving family.

CHAPTER 14

Moving On

W hen I look back at how all of this unfolded with the *accidental* meeting of my sister Marcia and me, I am filled with such gratitude that it is hard to put it into words. After having the opportunity to meet her on our first trip to Florida, going on trips to visit her in Arizona, trips to Sedona, having her come here to Nashville, and even making our sojourn to Clinton, Illinois, it is hard to imagine making it through my life without these experiences and time shared with her. Considering how unlikely these events were, I definitely believe that divine intervention was involved, and I certainly send up prayers of thanks for that often.

I do think often about the "what ifs" and the over-whelming likelihood of my sister and I never meeting. The biggest "what if" in this story is my birth mother's name showing up in my mailbox with the last name visible. Had that not happened, how would I have reacted to the standard, nonidentifying report I expected, simply to gather biological medical history and any social tidbits that were left in my file? Would I have decided that the original search was not enough, that I really wanted to find out who my biological parents were? Just as I surprised myself by my reaction to her maiden name being revealed to me, I was just as astounded by my immediate turnabout regarding wanting to meet my sister. What I'm trying to say is that I experienced some tipping points that allowed me to delve deeper into feelings that I honestly didn't know were there. Those little catalysts are what propelled me forward into more revealing searches, and I am, of course, immensely grateful for them. Can I candidly say that my search would have ended had the last name been whited out? No, I really cannot, because that wasn't the experience that I had.

Finding out that you have a sibling five decades into your life is definitely a different experience. There is a love that runs deep with many brothers and sisters, simply from growing up together in the same house with the same parents, experiencing all of life's ups and downs together. Some siblings remain close through adulthood, some do not. However, there is something to be said for the mutual experiences you shared growing up, whether it's sharing a bathroom for years, getting grounded together by your parents, or sharing Christmas together with your grandparents when they come to town. These, along with hundreds of thousands of other experiences, are what formed my relationship with my brother growing up, and every one of them, warts and all, are what make us siblings. I am very thankful for the opportunity to be Jamie's sister, which wouldn't have happened without the institution of adoption.

My regret that Marcia and I missed those first five decades together is so overshadowed by my thankfulness for what we now have that I can't be sad about times missed. I love my sister deeply, although that love has been forged over the last ten years rather than a lifetime. We already have memories of good times together. Thanks to Marcia, I have been able to catch up on my birth mother's life, her wonderful relationship with my sister, and what those intertwined lives entailed, including the places that they lived while Marcia grew up as well as many of their biggest life experiences. By graciously taking the time to reproduce family videos, send me many photos, and share my birth mother's entire journals, Marcia has handed me a gift of insight beyond comparison.

I was surprised at how profound my love for my sister became within weeks of the two of us making contact. We spent hours on the phone catching up on lost time as soon as Kim introduced us, but I felt this even before I'd met her in person a month and a half later. As human nature goes, it does seem odd to love someone so much when you haven't known them very long, but maybe it's just a genetic thing. Or maybe not. Perhaps it is just my appreciation for the biological connection that we have, which before her I had never shared with anyone of my generation or those before me. Whatever the source is, it really doesn't matter because that deep connection between my sister and me is there.

The keeping of secrets plays a substantive role in this story. Secrets may seem fairly inconsequential at the time; maybe it's just the easier way through a situation. But, as time goes on, and maybe you have a spouse or partner, children, even grandchildren, the secret dives even deeper, locked in a barricaded abyss. To bring it out years later could have the potential to ruin your marriage, your life, even your family's trust in you.

This is why I understand, from the depths of my heart, why Marti first decided to not tell her parents, and then to her dying day never told her husband, Marcia's dad. Same with Robert Stewart . . . if he chose to tell Kim Laube that he never had sex with Marti, it is not likely that he told his wife, his three children, or his grandchildren about "the baby."

The thing is, that's okay. Every human being on this planet has secrets: some that are eventually peeled back and revealed and others that remain locked up forever. Putting myself in either one of their shoes, I would find it exceedingly difficult to reveal news of a shrouded child years or decades later. Just like every one of us, their relationships with their closest loved ones hold the highest price. These connections are the core of our human experience.

So indeed, I understand. That is why the old adage holds a great deal of wisdom. Sometimes it's just better to let sleeping dogs lie.

Moses had two mothers: his birth mother and his adoptive one. Both of these women needed to be on this earth to create, protect, love, and nurture this child. Jochebed, his biological mother, carried him and gave birth to him during a very scary time to be giving birth to a male baby, since the pharaoh had given the command that all baby Hebrew boys should be killed. The pharaoh's daughter, who ironically became Moses's adoptive mother, found him floating in the Nile among the reeds where he had been planted in hopes of rescue. Without the actions of both women, Moses wouldn't have made it past infancy. To me, the takeaway from this is that it often takes more than one person to raise a child, and sometimes there's some divine influence involved.

I talk about accidents and mistakes several times throughout this story. When I was young, I believed that mistakes were just part of the human experience. As I've grown older, I no longer believe this to be the case. I think that all these events and adventures happen to us for a reason, intertwined with the rest of humanity for *their* express purposes as well. My adoption-search journey only strengthened that conviction and has allowed me to see how divine intervention is a very real part of our lives, especially if we choose to acknowledge it. If you haven't felt that way about your own life path, I encourage you to open your heart and see what happens. It's not just cliché—there truly are miracles happening around us every single day, not by accident.

During the course of writing this memoir, something very interesting related to our story was going on in the Iowa legislature (Iowa General Assembly). In early 2019, a bill had been introduced regarding access to a copy of an original birth certificate by an adult adoptee. Once again, Kim Laube, my incredible social worker, contacted me to tell me about this bill. By this time, she was no longer at Catholic Charities but continued to be actively involved in promoting the welfare of adoptees in many ways.

I had always been under the impression (and never told otherwise) that my "original" birth certificate that has been in our lockbox all my life was actually my only birth certificate, just the revised version of the original. The first time that I was old enough to look at my birth certificate, knowing that I was adopted, I found it interesting that the scribes simply eliminated the birth parents' names and plugged in the adoptive parents' names. Clearly, I understood the reasons for it being handled this way: my adoptive parents were now officially my parents and my birth parents had given up their rights.

But as literal as I have always been, to me a birth registration should document the specific event accurately rather than hiding, or altering, information for the protection of others. Under that line of thinking, the original birth certificate *does* exist; it's just likely that most adoptees don't realize it. The fact that there is an original birth certificate issued at birth and another one delivered at the adoption was something I knew nothing about until Kim Laube explained it to me when she first contacted me to tell me about this bill.

In May 2019, this bill, which would allow Iowa adoptees access to their original birth certificate, was passed in the Iowa Senate, but it did not pass in the Iowa House. In early February 2020, Senate Study Bill (SSB) 1040 passed its subcommittee, awaiting full Senate judiciary committee discussion. House Study

Bill (HSB) 226 also passed its subcommittee and went into full House committee discussion on February 24, 2021. I sent correspondence to each of the subcommittee members encouraging them to support this bill, because I feel strongly that adoptees should have at least some of the same civil liberties that their birth parents have had ever since adoption laws were established.

In an era when DNA tests are available to anyone who chooses to purchase them, the information regarding one's ancestors and living relatives has become exceedingly more accessible than in the past. As people view these results and see DNA relatives that are enough of a match to be first, second, or third cousins, or in some cases even siblings that they didn't know about, it seems that access to the factual details of one's birth becomes increasingly vital. Of course, the adoptee could always choose *not* to request their original birth certificate; it would just be nice for them to have the same liberties as the other individuals involved in the adoption process.

If you or anyone you know was adopted at birth, keep in mind that each state in the US has its own laws regarding access to original birth certificates. It is my understanding that, according to the American Adoption Congress, nine states currently allow adoptees who are over eighteen or twenty-one to access their birth certificates. In 2021 alone, around twelve states had bills in legislation that would allow adoptees to have access to their original birth certificates.

On April 13, 2021, the Birth Certificate Access Bill finally passed through the Iowa House of Representatives. This meant that now both the House and the Senate had voted unanimously to allow adoptees access to their original birth certificates. How did I find this out immediately? Once again, Kim Laube. She was actually there next to the governor when the bill was signed, and texted me shortly after. She is one incredibly thoughtful human being.

On the morning of April 14, I had my application to receive a copy of my original birth certificate notarized and in the mail less than twenty-four hours after the bill was passed. On May 19, 2021, HF855 was signed into law in the state of Iowa, giving adoptees born before 1971 access to their original birth certificates. Adopted people born after that year had to wait until January of 2022 to obtain this information, giving birth parents a window to redact their names from the birth certificate if they chose to do so. Birth parents could always file a redaction of their identifying information, as early as the time of their child's relinquishment; this just allowed them to have a six-month time period to redact now that the law had changed.

On June 30, 2021, the copy of my original birth certificate arrived in our mailbox, over sixty-one years after it was written. Of course, nowhere to be found on the document were the names and address of the parents who raised me, loved me, protected me, and told me I could do anything I put my mind to for over five decades. Present, however, was the name that I knew would be there, Margaret Jane Maurer. Her address on the certificate was a beautiful old house in Champaign, Illinois that still stands today, 203 N. Lynn Street. My birth mother lived on Lynn Street, and I was adopted by the Linns. What are the odds . . . one more little synchronicity?

Lines seven though eleven on the document were reserved for the name, age, birthplace, and occupation of the birth father. My heart raced as I plowed through the certificate to see if he was really on there.

It was blank. The entire father section was pure as the driven snow. Empty. Zilch. Vacuous.

Although I suspected that the birth father section might arrive blank, I wasn't really sure how I felt about that. I had done some research into how that was handled back in the 1950s and 1960s, and with "illegitimate" births (sheesh . . . doesn't that term seem brutally harsh nowadays?) the elimination of the father's name was fairly common. Seeing it empty also made me think about Marti getting her brother-in-law Bill involved from a legal standpoint. Although we have no idea what caused lawyers to get involved, that might be another reason why the birth father was not indicated on my original. Regardless, we will never know.

Being able to see and hold my original birth certificate after having it kept from me for over sixty-one years instilled a feeling deep within my soul that is difficult to describe. It's as though someone told you that your life started on October 17, 1959, when you *knew* there was a black hole for a month before that that no one would allow you to witness. Seeing the name, age, and address of the only biological relative that was present at my birth caused me to continue to stare at the certificate long after I had opened the envelope. Although I can't explain why, somehow, just seeing a copy of the actual certificate that documented my arrival on this earth gave me an immense sense of comfort. It is my life and I wanted to know my story from the beginning, from September 10, 1959. Although I don't have every little detail, I have enough, and in that I find great peace.

Acknowledgments

Thank you to my dear husband Dee (referred to throughout the book by his non-family name, Don) for putting up with *everything* related to writing this book during the last four years. The numerous ways that you helped me and provided emotional support go way beyond the call of the love-you-for-better-or-for-worse clause. Always with a smile on your face. You are my rock.

To my precious daughters, Lauren, Carolyn, and Kat, thank you for encouraging me to just write the dang thing when I kept talking about the story. Thanks for your input when I asked for it and thanks for the unending support. Doug, our master meat smoker, you too.

To my sister, Marcia, for being the other half of *our* story and for repeatedly answering my questions to make sure I got it all right. You are an extremely patient and loving human being.

To my cousin Jill Martin for having precision timing in visiting her dad, my Uncle Duane. Without your walking in and picking up that phone, who knows where this story would have gone. Or ended.

To the late Phyllis Langton, fellow author and happenstance neighbor, your constant cheerleading and telling me I could do it was nothing short of infectious. I miss having you in the next cul-de-sac every day when I walk by. In fact, I miss and love you so much that Dee and I adopted your precious mutt, Waltzing Matilda.

To my dear friends mentioned throughout this book . . . you each had a hand in building the blocks of this book whether you realized it or not. Even Fred, who called me an orphan.

My deepest gratitude to my dear friend, Stephanie Bodnar Ruez. You are my catalyst, who allows me to see things in a different light. You came along at the perfect time.

Thank you to my thoughtful friend, Karla Diehl, who pointed out an Arts and Business Council of Greater Nashville webinar that might give me some insight for the book I was finishing up. Thank you to Julie Schoerke Gallagher for being a speaker at that webinar and giving me the inspiration to take the plunge. Again, my gratitude goes out to Julie for hiring nothing but stellar employees. Elysse Wagner and Hannah Robertson, your constant support and enthusiasm (and patience) is beyond appreciated. Thanks also to Emily Colin and Anna Burdick for your superb editing grit; it's always a fun project when working on an author's first book!

Thank you, thank you, to Jennon Bell Hoffmann for your extraordinary insight and editing skills. When I first read through your content edit, I thought I was going to faint. Then I pulled myself up by the bootstraps and got to work again, knowing that I had been blessed with an editor who knew what she was talking about. Most people would call you an editor; I call you my Sherpa.

I extend eternal gratitude to Kim Laube for everything you did for me in this search for answers to the beginning of my life. Without your perseverance, many questions would have remained unanswered and the Road to Marcia would have remained incomplete. As well, thank you for fighting for the adoptees of Iowa and not giving up on that bill in the Iowa Legislature. I hope and pray that every state in our wonderful nation has their own "Kim" doing the same for them.

Finally, to the first social worker at Catholic Charities who forgot to white out my birth mother's last name, I cannot thank you enough. Maybe it was an *accident*, maybe it wasn't. Regardless, I am very, very grateful.

CPSIA information can be obtained
at www.ICGtesting.com
Printed in the USA
JSHW041809060722
27597JS00001B/55